KNIGHT-CAPRON LIBRARY
LYNCHBURG COLLEGE
LYNCHBURG, VIRGINIA 24501

UNDERSTANDING
GEORGE GARRETT

Understanding Contemporary
American Literature

Matthew J. Bruccoli, *Editor*

Understanding Bernard Malamud
  by Jeffrey Helterman
Understanding James Dickey
  by Ronald Baughman
Understanding John Hawkes
  by Donald J. Greiner
Understanding Thomas Pynchon
  by Robert D. Newman
Understanding Randall Jarrell
  by J. A. Bryant, Jr.
Understanding Edward Albee
  by Matthew C. Roudané
Understanding Contemporary American Drama
  by William Herman
Understanding Vladimir Nabokov
  by Stephen Jan Parker
Understanding Joyce Carol Oates
  by Greg Johnson
Understanding Theodore Roethke
  by Walter B. Kalaidjian
Understanding Mary Lee Settle
  by George Garrett
Understanding Isaac Bashevis Singer
  by Lawrence S. Friedman
Understanding Walker Percy
  by Linda Whitney Hobson

UNDERSTANDING
George
GARRETT

by R. H. W. DILLARD

UNIVERSITY OF SOUTH CAROLINA PRESS

ACKNOWLEDGMENTS

Grateful acknowledgment is made to the University of Arkansas Press for permission to reprint material from *The Collected Poems of George Garrett* (Copyright 1956, 1957, 1958, 1959, 1960, 1961, 1962, 1963, 1964, 1965, 1966, 1967, 1978, 1981, 1984 by George Garrett), and to George Garrett for his support of this project and his permission to reprint material from *For a Bitter Season* (Copyright 1956, 1957, 1958, 1959, 1960, 1961, 1962, 1963, 1964, 1965, 1966, 1967 by George Garrett) and other material.

Copyright © University of South Carolina 1988

Published in Columbia, South Carolina, by the
University of South Carolina Press

Library of Congress Cataloging-in-Publication Data

Dillard, R. H. W. (Richard H. W.), 1937–
   Understanding George Garrett / by R.H.W. Dillard.
     p.   cm. — (Understanding contemporary American literature)
   Bibliography: p.
   Includes index.
   ISBN 0-87249-550-7. ISBN 0-87249-551-5 (pbk.)
   1. Garrett, George P., 1929– —Criticism and interpretation.
I. Title. II. Series.
PS3557.A72Z64   1988
818'.5409—dc19   87-33403
                                                                                  CIP

CONTENTS

Editor's Preface

Chapter 1   Understanding George Garrett   1

Chapter 2   *The Finished Man*   34

Chapter 3   *Which Ones Are the Enemy?*   57

Chapter 4   *Do, Lord, Remember Me*   79

Chapter 5   The Elizabethan Novels: *Death of the Fox* and *The Succession*   112

Chapter 6   *Poison Pen*   163

Chapter 7   Poems and Short Stories   193

Conclusion   210

Bibliography   213

Index   221

EDITOR'S PREFACE

Understanding Contemporary American Literature has been planned as a series of guides or companions for students as well as good nonacademic readers. The editor and publisher perceive a need for these volumes because much of the influential contemporary literature makes special demands. Uninitiated readers encounter difficulty in approaching works that depart from the traditional forms and techniques of prose and poetry. Literature relies on conventions, but the conventions keep evolving; new writers form their own conventions—which in time may become familiar. Put simply, *UCAL* provides instruction in how to read certain contemporary writers—identifying and explicating their material, themes, use of language, point of view, structures, symbolism, and responses to experience.

The word *understanding* in the series title was deliberately chosen. Many willing readers lack an adequate understanding of how contemporary literature works; that is, what the author is attempting to express and the means by which it is conveyed. Although the criticism and analysis in the series have been aimed at a level of general accessibility, these introductory volumes are meant to be applied in conjunction with the works they cover. Thus they do not provide a substitute for the works and authors they introduce, but rather prepare the reader for more profitable literary experiences.

M.J.B.

UNDERSTANDING
GEORGE GARRETT

CHAPTER ONE

Understanding George Garrett

Career

George Garrett (born Orlando, Florida, 11 June 1929) has produced as large and significant a body of work as any writer of his generation, but it is probably also the most critically undervalued major work of that time. The author of six novels, seven books of poems, seven collections of short fiction, as well as plays, screenplays, and a varied body of critical writing (including a biography of James Jones and a study of Mary Lee Settle), Garrett has spent thirty years ranging widely among genres, examining his central thematic concerns while at the same time engaging in an exploration of the possibilities and limitations of literary conventions and forms. For example, he is the author of two historical novels of such complexity and imaginative vision that

2
UNDERSTANDING GEORGE GARRETT

Monroe K. Spears ranked them "in the exalted company of *Ulysses* and a very few other works that carry the novel form as far as it can go, exploiting all its resources and revealing new possibilities,"[1] while he is also the perpetrator of an outlandish satirical novel, *Poison Pen,* called by an anonymous reviewer a "brilliant, merciless, shapeless, many-layered, some splendored kazoo concerto."[2] Garrett has quite simply not limited the scope of his talents and interests sufficiently to allow himself to be categorized and "placed" by the American critical community.

After growing up in Florida and attending Sewanee Military Academy and the Hill School, Garrett went to Princeton, where he took his B.A. in 1952, the same year he married Susan Parrish Jackson. After service in the U.S. Army (field artillery) with two years overseas duty in Trieste and Austria, he returned to Princeton to take an M.A. in 1958. He finished all of his doctoral work except the dissertation and began a teaching career that has carried him with many stops from Wesleyan University to Hollins College, from the University of South Carolina to the University of Michigan.

He began to publish poems and stories in 1955, and his first collections, *The Reverend Ghost* (poems) and *King of the Mountain* (stories), appeared in 1957. In the next four years he estab-

UNDERSTANDING GEORGE GARRETT

lished himself as an important and prolific young writer by publishing five more books—three of them on the same day in 1961: *Abraham's Knife* (poems), *In the Briar Patch* (stories), and *Which Ones Are the Enemy?* (his second novel). His first novel, *The Finished Man* (1959), a story having to do with contemporary Florida politics, had gained him national attention as a leading new Southern writer, but his refusal to continue working in the same vein blurred that identification and caused *Which Ones Are the Enemy?* (an army novel set in Trieste) to gain less attention than its predecessor. When his third novel, *Do, Lord, Remember Me* (1965), appeared, its subject matter (the events surrounding a tent revivalist's visit to a small Southern town) made it too easily stereotyped, and the book was unfairly passed over as just another *Elmer Gantry*.

The publication of *Death of the Fox* (1971) gained him the widest critical attention and popular success of his career, and he followed that book in 1983 with another Elizabethan historical novel marked by revolutionary formal innovations, *The Succession*. (Princeton accepted those two novels as Garrett's dissertation and awarded him his doctorate in 1985.) His satirical novel, *Poison Pen*, appeared in 1986, and over the last two decades he has continued to publish collections of poetry and short fiction, including the comprehensive *The Col-*

lected Poems of George Garrett (1984) and *An Evening Performance: New and Selected Short Stories* (1985). He is presently Hoyns Professor of Creative Writing at the University of Virginia.

Overview

The great variety of form and content in the fiction and poetry of George Garrett may make it difficult for literary catalogers to classify and "place" him, but a careful reader of the body of work he has written over the last thirty years discovers quickly that it has genuine coherence and stability. Garrett's central concerns as well as his increasingly more complex methods of dealing with them are a direct result of his belief in the primacy of the "committed imagination" in art as well as in life. Whether a literary work is "realistic" or "utterly unrealistic," Garrett has said, "the truth of it . . . is essentially the same. It's the truth of the committed imagination. And in that sense, the commitment of the imagination, all good stories are true and autobiographical."[3] The writer is not engaged in an "assertion of self," but is rather committing his or her imagination to the demands of the work itself and to a truth which the writer both finds in the work and gives to it.

UNDERSTANDING GEORGE GARRETT

The result of this trust in the committed imagination is a body of work that is ruggedly independent of contemporary fashions and fads. His work is "committed," but it is not politically committed, as one might expect; *The Finished Man* is set in a Florida senatorial campaign, but Garrett does not "like to think of it as a political novel. . . . It is not primarily concerned with politics."[4] The basic rule that he set himself while writing *Death of the Fox* was "that in no way must this ever seem to be relevant to anything happening today, . . . that these people were different, and their problems were different."[5] In all of his work he has maintained a commitment to the creation and rendering of people and their problems as "different" and individuated, as humanly and spiritually rather than sociologically or politically relevant.

He has resisted literary fashions as well. His early stories were traditionally realistic and "well made," often strongly influenced by Hemingway; but even within the confines of his first story collection, *King of the Mountain*, he began to move away from that kind of story into the enigmatic parables of the "Comic Strip" sequence ("The Witness," "The Accursed Huntsman," and "How the Last War Ended") and the tough, anecdotal set of army stories grouped together as "What's the Purpose of the Bayonet?" His first novel, *The Finished*

Man, was also realistic and traditional in form, and it is often compared to Robert Penn Warren's *All the King's Men;* but the imaginative demands of his second novel, *Which Ones Are the Enemy?* required a colloquial, first-person narration so different from *The Finished Man* that Garrett's editor at Scribner's (who did not publish the book) is reputed to have accused him of turning in a friend's manuscript under his own name. Each story and each poem seems to require of Garrett's imagination its own specific telling, regardless of precedents in his own writing or the demands of literary fashion.

Using a multiple point of view reminiscent of Faulkner, *Do, Lord, Remember Me* not only takes a tent revivalist's Christian belief seriously, but also tells that serious religious story with a Chaucerian bawdiness and sexual directness so bold that its American publisher required that it be toned down before publication. In another unexpected change of direction Garrett then moved on to his first historical novel, *Death of the Fox,* a book which roused critics to call it "one of the best historical novels in years" (*Newsweek*), "a triumph of intellect and imagination" (*Saturday Review*), and "one of the finest novels we have ever read" (*Publishers Weekly*)—and this despite (and possibly because of) its rejection of most of the conventions of the

UNDERSTANDING GEORGE GARRETT

genre. As Garrett described it with tongue in cheek to a publisher, "To give you a clue as to how it goes, in the first 250 pages, the action may be summarized by saying that three people unbeknownst to each other have difficulty in getting to sleep."[6] Rather than use conventional narrative techniques to explore and tell his story, Garrett opted for an imaginative meditation on Elizabethan history centered upon and moving around the complex and paradoxical figure of Sir Walter Ralegh. As he said, the form developed from the commitment of Garrett's imagination to the radical otherness of the characters and events in his story.

Garrett's second Elizabethan historical novel, *The Succession*, is, as Monroe Spears has pointed out, a companion to its predecessor but a book which is very different, one which "has no hero . . . [but] insofar as it does, the hero has to be James, the villain of *Fox*."[7] It might be even more accurate to say that the book does not even have a central character, but instead a set of almost unrelated characters, with only the event of the succession of James to the throne of Elizabeth as its center; that it is not a meditation on Elizabethan history or the meaning of one man's life in his times, but rather a meditation on meaning itself, on time itself, on life itself.

At the same time that Garrett was working on

these two major historical novels whose seriousness, despite their comic moments, is indisputable, he was also writing a series of comic works about celebrity and the entangled mixture of reality, illusion, and unreality of modern public life. As early as the time when he was writing *The Finished Man*, Garrett had noticed and begun to commit his imagination to the growing two-dimensionality of American politics. As he mentioned to John Graham when discussing that novel: "Something has happened, we've become less dimensional. We are less direct; we have rapport with an image."[8] He began to extend that interest from the world of politics into the whole world of celebrity life in the group of poems concerning and often addressed to media sex goddesses and their handmaidens which appeared in *For a Bitter Season*; the poem "Celebrity Verses" satirizes both the women (Ann-Margret, Twiggy, Kim Novak, Barbara Steele, and Donna Michelle) and the general public's (and the poet's) fascination with them. The satirical novel *Poison Pen* is the fullest published expression of that strand of Garrett's imaginative commitment, taking as its target the full range of celebrity unreality; and although it is a full-length novel, it is only a small part of (and extension of) a massive unpublished novel on the subject, *Life With Kim Novak Is Hell*, a *roman maudit*

UNDERSTANDING GEORGE GARRETT

orts and shards of which have appeared in many small magazines as well as in the published novel.

The scope of Garrett's imaginative commitment is, then, unusually broad, ranging from the intensely personal meditations of many of the poems, to the classical satirical wit of other poems and epigrams; from studies of the struggles of and between pairs of people (fathers and sons, husbands and wives; soldiers, lovers) in the early stories, to full-length explorations of the lives of individuals in the worlds of politics, the army, and religion; from major imaginative re-creations of the different reality of Elizabethan lives, to violent and hilarious fictional assaults on the two-dimensionality of so much of modern life. His unrelenting search for literary forms capable of expressing that commitment has been equally widespread, pressing him forward in both his fiction and his poetry (and, for that matter, in his plays and screenplays) into areas of genuinely creative and radical form.

For all this variety of manner and matter, the key to an understanding of George Garrett's work lies not so much in that variety itself, but rather in the central body of belief which lies at the heart of it and makes it possible. Garrett is and always has been a Christian artist, drawing both his understanding of the nature and value of life and his aesthetic awareness from his belief. He is not a pietistic writer, wearing his belief on his sleeve or reverently reciting earlier Christian artists' words and ideas. As Charles Israel pointed out, "Garrett's Christian thought is complex. In some ways it is orthodox and formal. In other ways it is individual and inventive."[9] From this complex Christian thought arise Garrett's vision of the world and of human behavior in it, his major themes, and his aesthetic sense of the essentially enigmatic and parabolic nature of an imaginatively committed art.

The world of Garrett's poetry and fiction is the Christian fallen world: a world of unrelenting change, inevitable decay, unavoidable death; a world of sin in which vice and folly, lust and betrayal, sins deadly or merely degrading do not just afflict human beings but are of their very nature; a world in continual decline toward perpetual failure. It is a world in which, for better but more often for worse, the past remains actively present, either because of the actions of the ancestors which shape people socially, biologically, and individually, or because of the unattainably heroic standards which their lives and values seem to set for their descendants. "What can be said of the dead?" Garrett asks in his poem "Child Among

UNDERSTANDING GEORGE GARRETT

Ancestors," only to answer, "They rise / to make you curse the day that you were born."[10]

All of his fiction is set in this fallen world, and time and again Garrett defines that world directly in his poems: it is a world where "Trees reach up like drowning men / while worlds go turning to a bitter tune." ("Four American Landscapes" 43); where "We have lived too long with fear" ("For a Bitter Season" 14); where "I have to force / myself to vote, choosing among scoundrels" ("Main Currents of American Political Thought" 9); where "Flesh and spirit wrestle / and we call it love" ("Salome" 7). And yet a recognition of the fallen condition of this world is the first necessary step toward salvation, toward an understanding and acceptance that the fallen world is not the whole story, as Garrett has his Salome say:

> We couple like dogs in heat.
> We shudder and are sundered.
> We pursue ourselves,
> sniffing, nose to tail
> a comic parade of appetites.
>
> That is the truth,
> but not the whole truth (7).

It is the recognition that the bleakness of the fallen world is the truth but not the whole truth that enables the equally fallen human being to bless the day:

> To see suddenly and always the blue eye of God
> which greets his gasp with an enormous wink
> The river is burning and the gulls cry doom
> but the man of lead now smiles to discover
> that even his teeth are rich with silver and gold
> ("Maine Weathers" 49).

It is this double recognition and the gift of grace that allow the sinful believer, as Garrett does in the poem "Meditation on Romans," to pray aloud: "Yoke my shrugging shoulders, set upon my soul / (Thy will be done) the brightest crown of thorns."[11] It is this understanding that gives Ralegh the strength to command the executioner to strike at the end of *Death of the Fox* and which gives the drunken plowman out under the stars at the end of *The Succession* the impulse to wish a good night for Queen Elizabeth and the rest of the world "for the sake of our own sweet Jesus."[12]

The given moment in any of Garrett's works is always seen in the light of this double vision. It is no wonder, then, that he is drawn to central characters who might best be characterized as sinner-saints: people in whom the double vision of the world and their own double nature operate most fully. Sir Walter Ralegh in *Death of the Fox* and Big

UNDERSTANDING GEORGE GARRETT

Red Smalley in *Do, Lord, Remember Me* are the most obvious examples, sinners through whom God's voice speaks clearly and providence acts in the world. They are characters who, like Garrett's Salome, "had a dream of purity" and "have lived in the desert ever since" (7). Other less imposing characters like John Riche in *Which Ones Are the Enemy?* and numerous characters in the short fiction also belong to this group of sinner-saints. And most recently Garrett has admitted himself into the group at least indirectly in the complicated (and duplicitous) claims to (or disclaimers of) authorship of *Poison Pen* by himself and his scoundrelly character and dark double, John Towne, each of whom keeps taking the credit and putting the blame on the other. As Garrett admitted in an interview, "I've got to be in there, too. I'm just as much a dope as anybody else."[13]

Garrett's sense of the rich ambiguity of the double nature of human beings leads him to an admitted affection for the losers, those who have recognized their flawed natures and learned to live with them. W. R. Robinson noted that "to be man, his fiction implies, is to be finite and 'guilty'; it is to be a part of the world and responsible to it; it is to live in isolated individuality and with uncertainty and change as absolutes, yet care, as Garrett does so obviously, for all his fallen characters."[14]

14

UNDERSTANDING GEORGE GARRETT

Or, as the narrator of "Hooray for the Old Nth Field" (in the group of stories called "What's the Purpose of the Bayonet?") puts it:

"Save me from good people, on a piece of graphpaper, percentagewise. Give me the bottom of the barrel, men who still have themselves to laugh at and something real to cry about, who, having nothing to lose and being victims of the absurd dignity of the human condition, can live with bravado at least, and, if they have to die, can die with grace like a wounded animal."[15]

His personal awareness of human double nature is perhaps most clearly expressed in the poem "Luck's Shining Child," in which he presents himself as forced by being "broke again" to have his shoes resoled one at a time so that one is always "fat and slick with new leather" and the other always bears "a large hole like a wound." At the end of the poem he imagines (while trying not to) himself in his coffin in those shoes:

> one or the other a respectable brother
> and one or the other
>
> that wild prodigal whom I love
> as much or more than his sleek companion,
> luck's shining child (8).

UNDERSTANDING GEORGE GARRETT

Garrett's thoroughly Christian vision sees everyone as sinner-saint, some as luck's shining children, others as the luckless losers and prodigals, each capable of becoming the other, all loved despite the actions of luck or chance in their lives. The image of the goddess Fortuna haunts Garrett as much as it did the Elizabethans, and the only exorcism he finds is the same one they (for all their otherness) found: a trust in "our own sweet Jesus," a submitting to providence. The only villains in the works of Garrett are those who cannot see (or will not admit) their sinful natures, and he exposes their blindness and hypocrisy mercilessly. But, for all the compulsion he feels to excoriate vice and folly wherever he sees it, he never forgets that each of us "must be in there, too," each "as much a dope as anybody else."

The most significant action in a Garrett story or poem is, then, most likely to occur at a moment of self-discovery when limits are realized or the true double vision attained. "Garrett's favorite story," according to W. R. Robinson, "is an account of moral change, a fall from innocence into knowledge, begotten by a violence without evoking a violence within, of involvement in a power struggle from which there is no intellectual or moral escape."[16] These moments of discovery and change are often initiatory in Garrett's early fiction, in coming-of-age stories such as "The Rivals," "The Seacoast of Bohemia," "The Lion Hunter," and "The Last of the Spanish Blood," or in "King of the Mountain," in which a boy makes discoveries about the double nature of his heroic father. *The Finished Man* is concerned as much, or more, with Mike Royle's initiation into the modern world of two-dimensional politics and the elements of unreality in public life as it is about that world itself.

In Garrett's later works, when he became less interested in those particular initiations involved in growing up, the discoveries remain central; the world continues to reveal itself in surprising ways even to those who consider themselves fully initiated. He chose to close his retrospective collection of stories, *An Evening Performance*, with the short novel originally called "Cold Ground Was My Bed Last Night" but later renamed "Noise of Strangers." In it, in a small town appropriately named Fairview, a vagrant, the town sheriff, and his deputy all make discoveries about themselves that will change their lives permanently. The lives of these individuals repeat, in an almost allegorical way, both the primordial fall from innocence and the shift in Western consciousness from a pagan to a Christian world view. What they discover in Fairview will never allow them to turn back, to deny what they have learned, or ever to feel secure in

UNDERSTANDING GEORGE GARRETT

the same way again. Those kinds of discoveries are at the heart of Garrett's mature work: discoveries about the self and about the nature of life, discoveries of limitation, discoveries of life's increasing complexities, discoveries that can lead to new strength and understanding but which too often lead only to weakness and the creation of new illusions. And, of course, those discoveries occur in every life, in every family's life, in every community's life, and in every generation's life.

What makes the story of those moments of revelation so compelling in Garrett's work is his demonstration that discovery and understanding are so difficult to come by in a world in which truth and illusion are so inextricably intertwined. He believes with Northrop Frye that "a serious human life, no matter what 'religion' is invoked, can hardly begin until we see an element of illusion in what is really there, and something real in fantasies about what might be there instead."[17] Wisdom in such a world must be earned by hard experience and cannot easily be passed on to others. Garrett's stories about the love and necessary betrayals between fathers and sons express that difficulty, and in the poem "For My Sons," he tells his sons that "you have to learn / to spit in my face and save your souls." The only truth he can offer them is both painful to hear and has already been expressed in the Bible; still, it is all he has, and must be enough:

> Nothing of earned wisdom I can give you,
> nothing save the old words like rock candy
> to kill the taste of dust on the tongue.
> Nothing stings like the serpent, no pain greater.
> Bear it. If a bush should burn and cry out,
> bow down. If a stranger wrestles, learn his name.
> And if after long tossing and sickness you find
> a continent, plant your flags, send forth a dove.
> Rarely the fruit you reach for returns your love (69).

That the "earned wisdom" of this poem, both its undeniable value as well as the accompanying frustration that it is not more, is absolutely central to Garrett's thinking is further evidenced by his use of a version of this last stanza in the imaginary letter from Ralegh to his son in *Death of the Fox*, a letter which is at the heart of that novel. According to Garrett, the truth when it is earned is hard truth, and the telling of it even harder.

How the individual survives and manages to live honestly and well in a world in which truth is both so hard to take and so hard to acquire is the central moral problem Garrett addresses in his work. For one who had "a dream of purity" but must live now in a desert of harsh truth and pervasive lies, the answer must necessarily be both diffi-

UNDERSTANDING GEORGE GARRETT

cult and pragmatic. The question must, however, be answered, and for the simple reason stated by the theologian Karl Barth in a passage which Garrett used as the epigraph for the concluding section ("Fig Leaves") of his third book of poems, *Abraham's Knife:* "If we had our first wish would we not turn away from life and society in utter skepticism and discouragement. But whither? From life and society one cannot turn away. They surround us on all sides; they set questions for us; they confront us with decisions. We must hold our ground."[18]

In the poem "Fig Leaves," Garrett faces the problem bitterly and directly. The poem begins with the speaker "sick of the dishonesty of men" and:

> sick unto death of myself
> and the lies I tell myself, waking, walking,
> sleeping, dreaming, lies that must choke
> and gag me like a drunk man's vomit.

But that disgust is finally resolved by a recourse to biblical truth and to a clear-eyed recognition of what people are and must do:

> Better our sole flag were fig leaves
> at least to salute the mercy of God
> when in the cool of the evening He came

> (Adam and Eve on trembling shanks
> squatted and hoped to be hidden)
> and cursed us out of the garden.
> But not before we learned
> to wear our first costume
> (seeing the truth was a naked shame),
> to lie a little and live together (68).

The dream of individual purity must necessarily be rejected in order to live in the world of lies, enabling one then to recognize the importance even of the lie as a functional part of the truth of a world in which people must live *together.*

It is this living in the world that the imagination supports and, indeed, makes possible. To live by abstractions (the dream of purity) in the world of lies is to be unable to recognize the truth either about oneself or those with whom one lives. "People out there in the streets are living and dying for *abstractions,*" Garrett said in an interview in 1969.

> And I don't think anybody would shoot a gun at anybody else, no matter what side they're on, if they could imagine vividly what a bullet does. I think they'd throw the gun away. . . . Perhaps the only way we as writers are able to do any good is through the development of the human imagination. The aesthetic experience of any kind cultivates the imagination, which has been stultified by abstractions.[19]

UNDERSTANDING GEORGE GARRETT

This may seem a limited way "to do any good" in this violent world, but it is the writer's "only way," and the limitation does not negate the significance of what is accomplished. Karl Barth may offer yet another key to understanding George Garrett when he says (in the same essay from which Garrett took his epigraph), "However true it may be that everything we do within the limits of mere particular things and events is only *play* in relation to what should be done, it is none the less *significant* play if it is rightly engaged in."[20]

This necessary rejection of the dream of purity is essential not only to Garrett's moral understanding, but also to his aesthetics, to the method and manner of his art as well as to its matter. If the truth in life must be discovered and dealt with in such a complex way, then the truth of an art of committed imagination must be attained in a way equally complex. Garrett's Salome describes her dance in this way:

> All the world knows
> truth is best revealed
> by gradual deception.
> It was a striptease pure and simple.[21]

The "gradual deception" of Garrett's art, "striptease" though it may in one way be, is, however, never "pure and simple." It may better be described as enigmatic and parablelike. "It is part and parcel of our whole Western tradition," Garrett has said, "that the truth is somehow contained in a parable which is in and of itself a beautiful lie."[22] The "significant play" of art, the lie of art, is, then, a saving lie, one which enables us to face the "naked shame" of the truth and to live with it.

Garrett's reference to the traditional Western view that truth may be stated in the beautiful lie of a parable reveals the strong influence on his aesthetic thought of St. Augustine, especially as interpreted by D. W. Robertson, Jr., the brilliant medievalist with whom Garrett studied at Princeton. Augustine's defense of "poets from those who say that they write lies" is that "a feigned fable which refers to a true *significatio* [meaning] is not a lie," and that in fact "those things which are said figuratively in the Scriptures move and inflame love more than those things which are said literally."[23] The "enigmas" of parable and all parablelike art seem, to Augustine and to Garrett, to function better in the world of lies than statements of the naked truth. "Paradoxically, there is a sense in which 'enigmas' are more readily understood than literal statements, for an unusual configuration of 'things which are known' stimulates the perception of an abstract unknown."[24] In Garrett's poem "Angels," he examines the enigma of those

> things so beautiful
> and strange my mind can't hold
> them though it wrestle.

He thinks of Caedmon (the seventh-century English poet whom he has mentioned more than once as an influence and literary hero), who responded to the angel's song with beautiful and expressive song of his own; but, aware as always of his double nature, Garrett also thinks of Jacob, "who choked / an answer from his angel." He concludes the poem by emphasizing his place in the fallen world of lies and affirming the saving role of parablelike art:

> I go alone and anxiously
> remembering that truth is the center
> of all fables and, fabulous,
> the lightning of love
> creates the angel and the wrestler.
> Translate this parable.
> It means to praise (55).

The lie of art is the best path to truth in the world of lies, or, at the least, it is the only effective way to communicate truth in a world in which we must learn "to lie a little and live together." It enables a person to perceive that which he or she cannot know and praise that "which the mind can't hold."

The paradox that the stuff of Garrett's fiction and poetry is so palpably realistic and grounded in the things of this world, while that work is at the same time rooted aesthetically and philosophically in enigma and parable, should come as no surprise and offer no problem to a reader who remembers the parables of Christ, which are so realistically and so plainly told—and so extraordinarily complex, involving, and demanding of active interpretation. Barth's description of the method of the parables, of "form which issues from an inner necessity," applies as well to Garrett's work: "This view of life conceives the happenings of the day to be in their way fully justified, inevitable, and complete. . . . Only out of the keenest consciousness of redemption can one represent life as it is—as Jesus did."[25] In neither his poetry nor his fiction does Garrett (as has so often otherwise been the case since the aesthetic revolution of his modernist predecessors) make the empty landscapes and events of this world seem new and significant only by giving them metaphorical overtones of human archetypal dreams, myths, and faiths; rather, he gives his faith and "consciousness of redemption" tangible life and relevance by clothing them in the "fully justified, inevitable, and complete" things of this real world, by incarnating idea in fact. Faith creates a center which does hold.

A good introduction to both the parablelike quality of Garrett's work and his aesthetic vision is the short story "An Evening Performance." Often comic in tone but at the same time completely serious, the story concerns the coming to a small town of:

> ONE OF THE FABULOUS
> WONDERS OF MODERN TIMES
> STELLA THE HIGH DIVER
> SHE DIVES ONE HUNDRED FEET
> INTO A FLAMING CAULDRON (3)

The show is put on by an unlikely troupe of three people: Stella, the diver, who is mute; her unnamed manager, "an angry little man with a limp" (4); and Angel, a frail little girl who always wears white, with "unlikely eyes and hair as bright as new pennies" (5). They have come to hustle the town at two bits a ticket, but they are in turn hustled by the town—forced to buy a license they cannot afford and therefore forced to deal away half their take to a local businessman who pays for the license. On the evening of the performance the

UNDERSTANDING GEORGE GARRETT

businessman (using the threat of having them arrested for fraud) makes Stella dive, even though she doesn't want to because of dangerous windy and rainy conditions. She climbs the tower and, without further ado, dives into a blazing tank of water (and gasoline) that's barely six feet deep. Although the businessman and the crowd demand more, that is the whole act, and the next morning the troupe is gone except "for the dark spots on the grass where the flaming water had splashed, except for a few posters remaining (and they were not true to fact or life)" (11). That, briefly, is the plot of the story; it gains its parablelike richness from the texture of its telling and from its brief description of the lingering effects of the performance on the lives of the townspeople.

The story is filled with biblical echoes: for example, the tower on the poster rises into the clouds "like Jacob's dreamy ladder" (3); the manager stopped in at the Paradise Diner when he was putting up the posters; a reference is made to "wise men of the East" (9); Stella's robe drops from the tower like a snake—a mixture of positive and negative images appropriate to her dive into a lake of fire. And it becomes quite clear that the three visitors are a reference to the three angels who visited Abraham at Mamre; Stella, whose name means "star," speaks only with "hands as swift as wings" (5), and, of course, the child is named Angel. The lame man insists that there is nothing magical or dreamlike about Stella's dive, that it is "skill, skill pure and simple, . . . the living and breathing proof of the boundless possibility of all mankind" (9-10); but, although the story is not allegorical or limited to a strictly religious interpretation, it is nonetheless a fictive fleshing out of the biblical injunction, "Let brotherly love continue. Be not forgetful to entertain strangers: for thereby some have entertained angels unaware."[26]

The manager claims that Stella's dangerous dive "should make you happy. It should make you glad to be alive" (10), but its effects on the town are far more varied. Preachers denounce it as the work of the devil; drunkards and tellers of tall tales mythologize it "until the legend . . . was like a beautiful tapestry before which they might act out their lives, strangely dwarfed and shamed" (11-12); and children yearn to know when the three will come again. A wise man says it was a terrible thing, a fall from innocence into sophistication, ruining their appreciation of ordinary marvels, requiring "a regular apocalypse to make us raise our eyebrows again"—to which Garrett adds, "He was almost right, as nearly correct as a man could hope to be" (12). And, most important, and what the wise man cannot even imagine, "more than one aging, loveless woman slept better ever after, smiled as she dreamed herself gloriously descending for all the world to see from a topless tower into a lake of flame" (12).

The difficult and dangerous evening performance operates, then, as an angelic visitation, a revelation, a parable, and (like the story itself) a parabolic work of fiction. It is an act that transforms the imaginative life of the town, that creates new insight which perhaps only the apocalypse can ultimately satisfy, that opens a window on an eternity in which even the lake of flame (into which Satan and his followers shall be cast) may be mastered and transformed. The truth of the "beautiful lie" of the story is revealed by "gradual deception," and the "abstract unknown" becomes perceptible in the motley garb of an enigmatic but comically realistic present day, a very fallible and human present day in which both the truth and its reception are difficult to understand and are ultimately available only to the imagination of the alert and serious reader.

This vital tension in Garrett's work between an imaginative commitment to a realistically rendered world and an equally strong commitment to an art of parable and enigma has led him necessarily on

UNDERSTANDING GEORGE GARRETT

a quest for forms sufficiently radical to express his increasingly more complex vision. His poetry has moved from dynamically compressed formal modes, with ever-increasing experimentation in form and content, toward open forms, more daring uses of colloquial language, and what Charles Israel aptly describes as "unselfconscious humor."[27] The fiction, too, has evolved from the relatively traditional realism of the early stories and *The Finished Man* to the metafictional complexities of *The Succession* and *Poison Pen*, in which the form of the text itself is as important to the work's meaning as the story it tells; from (to use Umberto Eco's terms) "closed texts" which require essentially passive and predetermined reader response to "open texts" which demand active reader participation and involvement; from "the text that tries to fulfill the wishes of the readers already to be found in the street" to "the text that seeks to produce a new reader."[28]

According to Garrett, "There is a *conversation* that goes on in an unbroken way between the reader and the writer. If the book is any good, and he's hooked on it, he's bringing something in. . . . There's . . . a real copulative spirit going in the reading experience."[29] The writer's obligation is to establish that "copulative spirit," to enlist the reader in the creation of the text, fully aware of his or her role in that activity. "There are books that can engage you so that you don't want to go to work or something, that's true, but you know you're reading a *book*." He goes on to say, recognizing, with Eco, that this conscious act of writing and reading the text, this "conversation," is the vital heart of the "any good" that people, as writers and readers, can "do"; it is, in its freeing of the imagination, a moral action of great force and power.

Garrett's steady movement toward increasingly more "open" texts is integral to his lifelong effort to engage the reader in that active "conversation." The delight he once expressed in "all the ramifications" of Christ's explaining the parable of the sower to his disciples, and his recognition that "the whole parable in itself is the story of the disciples' wanting to know what it means,"[30] offer further evidence of the importance he gives to the "conversation" itself as well as to the subject of that conversation. Any understanding of his later work, and particularly *The Magic Striptease*, *The Succession*, and *Poison Pen*, depends heavily on an awareness of Garrett's determination to "produce a new reader" capable of sharing actively in that significant conversation with the properly generative "copulative spirit."

UNDERSTANDING GEORGE GARRETT

Understanding George Garrett requires, then, an alertness to both text and texture, a willingness to participate actively in the workings of the fully committed imagination, and an awareness of the complexity and richness of Garrett's Christian thought. His open-eyed examination of the moral life in the dark world of lies is genuinely profound and moving, and his comic vivisection of the vice and folly of that same world is equally, if hilariously, profound. The body of his work is large, and exploring its truth and its gradual deceptions and revelations is an exciting and valuable experience, pure and simple.

Notes

1. Monroe K. Spears, "George Garrett and the Historical Novel," *Virginia Quarterly Review* 61 (1985): 276.
2. *Kirkus Reviews* 1 Apr. 1986.
3. John Graham and W. R. Robinson, "George Garrett Discusses Writing and His Work," *Mill Mountain Review* 1 (1971): 81.
4. Graham and Robinson 84.
5. James J. McAuley, "A Panel on the Novel," *Mill Mountain Review* 1 (1971): 140–141.
6. John Carr, *Kite-Flying and Other Irrational Acts: Conversations with Twelve Southern Writers* (Baton Rouge: Louisiana State University Press, 1972) 178.
7. Spears 270.
8. Graham and Robinson 85.

UNDERSTANDING GEORGE GARRETT

9. Charles Israel, "George Garrett," *American Poets Since World War II.* Vol. 5 of *Dictionary of Literary Biography;* ed. Donald Greiner (Detroit: Bruccoli Clark / Gale, 1980) 265.

10. *The Collected Poems of George Garrett* (Fayetteville: University of Arkansas Press, 1984) 17. Further reference to poems will be to this edition unless otherwise noted and will be noted parenthetically.

11. George Garrett, *For a Bitter Season* (Columbia: University of Missouri Press, 1967) 107.

12. Garrett, *The Succession* (Garden City: Doubleday, 1983) 538.

13. Carlos Santos, "U. Va. Professor Tweaks the Trends," *Richmond Times-Dispatch* 28 Dec. 1986: 1.

14. W. R. Robinson, "The Fiction of George Garrett," *Red Clay Reader* 2 (1965): 16.

15. Garrett, *An Evening Performance: New and Selected Short Stories* (Garden City: Doubleday, 1985) 33. Further references to short fiction will be to this edition unless otherwise noted and will be noted parenthetically.

16. Robinson 16.

17. Northrop Frye, *The Great Code: The Bible and Literature* (New York: Harcourt Brace, 1982) 50.

18. Garrett, *Abraham's Knife* (Chapel Hill: University of North Carolina Press, 1961) 43.

19. Carr 195.

20. Karl Barth, *The Word of God and the Word of Man* (New York: Harper, 1957) 308.

21. Garrett, *For a Bitter Season* 15. The last line does not appear in the collected edition of the poems.

22. McAuley 139.

23. D. W. Robertson, Jr., *A Preface to Chaucer* (Princeton: Princeton University Press, 1962) 59, 56.

24. Robertson 57.

25. Barth 304-5.

26. Hebrews 13:1-2. Garrett added these verses as an epigraph to the story in the collected edition of the stories (1).

27. Israel 269.

28. Umberto Eco, *Postcript to The Name of the Rose* (New York: Harcourt Brace, 1983) 48–49. See also Umberto Eco, *The Role of the Reader* (Bloomington: Indiana University Press, 1979).
29. Carr 195.
30. McAuley 139.

CHAPTER TWO

The Finished Man

The coherence and stability of the entire body of George Garrett's work is such that it comes as no surprise to discover that perhaps the best introduction to his first novel, *The Finished Man,* is a poem written two decades after that book. The poem, "Main Currents of American Political Thought," addressed to Garrett's late grandfather, is both a meditation on change and the relentless passage of time, and an indictment of "these bitter, shiny times," particularly of the devolution which Garrett believes to be occurring in American political life.

The poem is built upon lists of things now gone that Garrett associates with his grandfather: first, possessions—demitasse cups and cigars, the farm with its turkeys and chickens, its cows and "the dead Pierce Arrow" in the barn, furniture, a service pistol and elephant gun, "the great bland

THE FINISHED MAN

moosehead on the wall"; then, objects of belief—
the free public schools and the petit jury which his
grandfather believed "will keep / the democratic
spirit of this country alive," but which Garrett feels
"are going, too"; and, finally, family—the grandfather's five sons and three daughters, "all dead or
dying slow and sure," with even the grandchildren
"riddled with casualties." "You would not believe
these bitter, shiny times," the poem concludes:

> What became of all that energy and swagger?
> At ninety you went out and campaigned
>   for Adlai Stevenson
> in South Carolina. Half that age and I have to force
> myself to vote, choosing among scoundrels.[1]

The idea that a certain substantiality has gone
out of American political life, both "energy and
swagger," to be replaced only by images and illusions, by cowardice and blandness, is central to
The Finished Man and to Garrett's political and social thought. That this loss is not limited to political life or even to American life the poem makes
clear by associating those kinds of losses with the
inevitable losses of life itself, its "casualties" and
its "dying slow and sure." Endemic to life is loss,
and the vanity of human wishes remains the hard
and central truth of the fallen world of lies.

UNDERSTANDING GEORGE GARRETT

These ultimate losses and the victories that are still possible despite them find expression in the novel in the more limited losses and gains of a modern Florida political campaign, one which delineates with particular clarity Garrett's view of the growing two-dimensionality of modern public life. Garrett comments:

I suppose one of the things that I felt at the time that I was doing the book is that once upon a time, perhaps not so long ago in a nostalgic America which may never have existed, there was a more direct rapport with the voter and a personality. Somewhere in there I made a thing about how the faces of the average run of the mill politician in the Brady photographs are wild-looking to us today. The whole make-up of the face—they would be strange people. And these were ordinary politicians. Something has happened, we've become less dimensional. We are less direct; we have rapport with an image.[2]

In the novel an aging, homely representative of the old politics, a New Dealer from the Depression years, is matched against a young, handsome representative of the new generation. The face of the incumbent, Senator Allen Parker, is exaggerated and remarkably expressive in direct encounters, as, for example, during a speech which opens the novel: "He started with a joke. . . . As they

THE FINISHED MAN

laughed his face changed. His mouth tightened and turned down. The high angle of his cheekbones, the soft hound's eyes, the thicket of unruly hair, the ruddy, splotched complexion became no longer clownish, but, in a wink of time, the rude composite pieces of a tragic mask."[3] But, Garrett noted in an interview, "the thing that worked for the Senator doesn't work anymore. What was once his individual character is now 'he is not as good looking.' "[4] His opponent and former assistant and protégé, John Batten, is, on the contrary, "smooth as a polished stone" (145). Mike Royle, the central character of the novel, a young man working for Senator Parker, sees him as a very modern and ordinary American type:

John Batten's type wasn't regional; rather, since uniformity defined it, he was a man to be found most anywhere in the country today like the popular, attractively packaged foods available in supermarkets from Taos, New Mexico to the windblown coast of Maine. To Mike the type seemed to be the final product of our culture, our education and our ideals. He had been molded as neatly as a lead soldier. The only difference between a John Batten in Detroit and a John Batten in Tallahassee (and *that* difference, too, would be weakened now by the ever-spinning lathe of standardization) would be the special manners of the particular place (145).

UNDERSTANDING GEORGE GARRETT

One of the ironies of the novel is that this ultimate inheritor of both Southern traditions (by way of his mentor Senator Parker's enigmatic blend of Old and New South values) is himself so lacking in regional characteristics. He is the final product of a media-defined culture that is rapidly erasing all specifically regional characteristics while producing a national image of how the political leader should appear and, thus, what he should be.

It is immediately after his recognition of Batten's nature that Mike thinks of the politicians' faces in the old Brady photographs and realizes that "those pictures and his indivisible feelings about them may have had much to do with his sudden whim to leave his job and to come home and work for Allen Parker" (146). Mike is the younger son of another politician, Judge Joseph Royle, who becomes a third candidate in the race (duped by Batten and his own ambition). Before the story and the election are over, Mike will learn much about all three candidates and about appearance and reality in general, and he speaks for Garrett in his distrust and disapproval of political and public imagery as a replacement for personal belief, commitment, and character. This disapproval eventually evolved into the scathing political satire of *Poison Pen*.

The campaign itself is as complex and famil-

THE FINISHED MAN

iarly simple as all political campaigns are. Senator Parker plans to retire and allow his protégé Batten a clear path to the senatorial nomination; but when he discovers that Batten is being supported by the people who have always opposed him, he realizes that he "had erred in imagining a kind of reincarnation of himself (the original sin of fathers), that this man, trained and cultivated, educated for the job, would follow the way that he had gone" (52). Parker double-crosses Batten and announces his candidacy for reelection. Despite his son's warnings, Judge Royle, an old populist New Dealer himself, is used by Batten as a stalking horse to draw votes from Parker's constituency. Even after he realizes what has happened, he continues on, gaining for himself the praise of editorialists and even the Governor (who is thinking ahead to a future race for the senate himself) as the "moral" candidate, the conscience of the bitter fight.

The strain is, however, too much for him, and Judge Royle dies suddenly and unexpectedly; but Parker's campaign is in too much trouble even for that to help. Parker has by that time rejected the advice of his old advisers and turned in desperation to his new public relations assistant, Vivian Blanch, who has advised that he bring race into the campaign to win the remnants of the Ku Klux

UNDERSTANDING GEORGE GARRETT

Klan vote. The last chance that Parker has to tell the truth and regain the honesty of his campaign is foiled when a young black man attempts to assassinate Parker but instead kills a mayor who is also on the platform, causing an atmosphere of racial tension, hatred, and fear to grip the state. Batten wins the election; Parker sinks into an almost surreal despair but immediately bounces back and plays the Good Loser (thinking ahead to the next gubernatorial election); and the political world continues, perhaps less "dimensional" than before but essentially unchanged. It remains, in Senator Parker's words, "entirely a world of appearances, of two tight little dimensions" in which "your life's like a game of cards" (53).

The shape of the campaign defines the shape of the novel, but it remains "a kind of . . . theatrical background against which these characters played."[5] The novel opens with the attempted assassination, then shifts back in time to Mike Royle's joining the Parker campaign just before the Senator's public announcement that he is going to run. The real story of the novel is the story of Mike Royle's coming of age, his initiation into the duplicitous and difficult realities of life in the world of lies, and his learning how to live as truly as possible in it.

Several of Garrett's short stories of this period

THE FINISHED MAN

have to do directly with initiatory experiences, of boys and of young men, and they are more often than not linked directly to *The Finished Man*, either by sharing with that book characters from one side or the other of Mike's family or by containing material which Garrett worked into the novel. Among these stories are "The Seacoast of Bohemia," "A Hard Row to Hoe," and the title story from *King of the Mountain*, the volume in which all three stories were collected, as well as some material Garrett was later to use in "Lion," a story in *In the Briar Patch*. Almost the entire story "King of the Mountain" appears in the novel, and in some ways it contains the shape and meaning of the larger work in microcosm.

In the story a boy witnesses his father's humiliation (and a vicious, crippling physical beating) at the hands of the Ku Klux Klan: "Not those men in sheets, crackpot fanatics, you can joke about now or piously deplore, but a ruthless political machine, a club for the lost and lonely, the embittered and the discontented. They had the county and a lot of the state and they meant to keep what they had."[6] He also watches the strain between his mother and his father, the one a daughter of an Episcopalian old Georgia family fallen on hard times, the other a Baptist, a Florida cracker who read the law and became a lawyer, and who "being self-educated . . . believed in some few things with an unsophisticated tenacity" (17). After the beating the father buys a pistol, but the mother asserts her authority in the house and forces him to throw it away; she cannot, however, persuade him to move away or give up his fight with the Klan.

The boy, realizing how miserable his mother, with her memories of her comfortable and sophisticated upbringing, must be in this poor little town, overhears a quarrel in which his father asserts his position as the person whose work enables her father to live graciously: "He's a fine old gentleman by grace of me" (20). As his mother weeps over her piano, the boy goes outside and climbs a mulberry tree where he "looked all around, as high and proud and lonely as the king of the mountain, and nobody, nobody would dare to come and pull him from his perch" (20). The rest of the story draws the boy metaphorically out of the tree and down from the mountain into the world where he must abandon his dream of purity and live in the desert of the world for better and for worse.

The family dog is shot by the town's chief of police, and the father turns that into an occasion for a fiery, populist speech which leads directly to his election to the first of many public offices, in-

THE FINISHED MAN

cluding senator and governor. The celebration of his victory has an almost mythic quality to it, "the once-in-a-blue-moon flavor of the celebration that follows the slaying of a dragon" (29). The boy witnesses it all and sees the double nature of his father clearly, concluding sadly years later "that it took a narrow-minded, petty demagogue with a wild desire to be a martyr to stand up for law and order at that time." (29). The narrator of the story argues for the necessity and importance of the father's actions, but the boy can only hate him without knowing why—and, in the original version of the story, doesn't even "know for sure whether I hate him or not."[7]

Many of the conflicts that haunt Mike Royle in the novel are present in the story: the double nature of the individual, the tensions between Old South culture and values and New South strength and action, the manipulative techniques needed to achieve the good in a democratic society, the struggle of a family to maintain its love despite the strains and contradictions of family life, the absolute need for a witness to become an actor if he is to live effectively in the world and not above it (or unable to understand his relationship to it). The boy, like it or not, must come down from the tree and deal with all of those conflicts within himself.

In the version of the story which appears in

The Finished Man, the father becomes Judge Royle, elected judge in his first campaign but doomed to fail at his tries for higher office. The boy becomes Mike's older brother Jojo, a disillusioned and even cynical drifter who, after a variety of jobs and a stint as a fighter pilot in the Second World War, settles in a nearby town as a disc jockey on an all-night radio station, refusing to come home, struggling to free himself from his family and his confused alliances, "but in truth still webbed, still tightly tied to all his past" (38). Jojo leaves home but never escapes it; his sister Mary Ann never leaves; his brother Mike leaves home, marries, divorces, comes home to work for Senator Parker, and thereby comes to terms with his past and himself. For Mike, going back is, as W. R. Robinson suggested, "a prerequisite for his going on."[8] At the end of the novel Jojo remains caught in the trap of his life, too clear-eyed to ever escape, to learn to "lie a little and live together." Mary Ann, however, leaves home for a trip to Rome, and Mike stays at home but transforms it and his life by agreeing to defend the young black man who killed the mayor while attempting to kill Senator Parker.

The three main parts of the novel are entitled "Beginning: Witness," "Middle: Victim," and "End: Actor," and they parallel Mike's growth as a

THE FINISHED MAN

moral individual. In order to come through his experience whole, to be able to act (both to play his role and to act morally), Mike must first come to terms with the essential doubleness of human beings and of life. Early in the novel he decides that his father must at some time have been remarkably innocent. "Otherwise how to explain his deep hurt when he was gored on the horns of appearance and reality? Otherwise what cause for the biblical ferocity, real or merely reputed, of his justice?" (67). Mike decides that he must have inherited the trait and his father's view of the doubleness of human experience:

That, it seemed, was the whole fruit, crop, of his father's experience, reduced to its lowest common denominator, its simplest factor, the knowledge, that every thoughtful child carries in his head like a gyroscope, that the whole world is double, that there is one that we look at and that looks back at us, and neither is true and both are alien, castled, like snails, in enigma (66–67).

Dealing with the enigma is, however, more difficult than merely recognizing it. Both the Judge and his alienated son Jojo have, in their radically different ways, accepted that hopeless attitude toward human failing. The Judge raises pigs, and he uses pigs as a metaphoric base for his position when he suggests that pigs are exactly what they are, without pretense or hypocrisy and that God must have loved pigs when he made them:

> Now a man, a man walks on two legs, and it says in the Bible that he's in the image of God. He shaves every day and he takes a bath every now and then. This side of the jungle we don't eat each other up any more. And for all of that a man is dirtier, and wallows in more shit and mire than any pig ever dreamed of. The stink of man—once you get your nose trained to detect it—is the foulest thing in creation (60).

Mike, for all his recognition of his affinities with his father, thinks that he is superior to this dark view of human nature, and that sense of superiority is the key to his distance from events, his ability to be a witness and not a participant. But Vivian Blanch defines Mike in quite a different way. Vivian is the spokesperson in this novel for illusion and dishonesty, for image rather than substance, for a monocular view of reality that is as cynical (and probably more cynical) than the Judge's view at its bleakest. She is a great fan of striptease and uses it as her central metaphor for truth. Unlike Salome, whom she relegates to the category of "*historical*, for God's sake" (130), Vivian does not recognize that there is more to truth than "the plain truth." She does not suffer like

THE FINISHED MAN

Salome, but delights in her striptease version of appearance and reality:

So what's the naked truth? I'll tell you. Nothing! Nothing at all. A naked woman is nothing but skin and meat and bones. If one of these women just walked out here naked and stood there, there wouldn't be anything to it. Just one more naked woman. But—don't you see?—you get colored lights, you have music, you put on a costume and you strip in a kind of dance. You take it off a little bit at a time. The style is everything. You *create* something. You create the naked truth while you're trying to find it. It wasn't there before, but now it is. It's magnificent. It's mystical (130).

When Mike is unable to share her understanding and finds himself unable to speak to her of his wife and his divorce, she puts him in his place, tells him to realize that he is not just a witness to life: "You're not really one of *us*. You're not really one of the chosen people—the spectators. You know what you are? You're just another godamn victim in disguise" (132).

Later, Mike finds himself much more involved, sexually and emotionally, with Vivian, "tossed on the horned duplicity of contradictory emotions, . . . fascinated and repelled," and he decides that "reality was for her, indeed, a perpetual striptease, a dance of innumerable veils. Therefore appearance was all" (169). But even Vivian is more complex than Mike thinks, and what he discovers about her wounded and distorted sexuality, along with what he learns about his father, Senator Parker, and even John Batten, forces him to recognize the accuracy of Vivian's analysis of his condition, that he is "just another godamn victim."

Mike's discovery of the weaknesses and double natures of his father and of his surrogate father, Senator Parker, radically shakes his confidence in himself and his whole world. His father's pride and ambition, as Mike saw, allowed even that cynical and focused old man to be hoodwinked and ultimately to be driven to his death in a vain and essentially selfish campaign. Parker, on the contrary, had always seemed a fascinating enigma to Mike, the type of "his regional tradition: the inevitable tension between the strong ideals of a democratic society and the ingrained dream of a natural aristocracy" (45). But when he reveals himself also to be capable of using racist tactics to win an election, to deal with the Ku Klux Klan, to lie to those closest to him as well as to the voters, to drink himself into a stupor rather than face the hard truth of his campaign, Mike realizes that even a recognizably enigmatic human being is far more complex than he had ever imagined. Both his father and Senator Parker are in some sense "fin-

THE FINISHED MAN

ished" men, but Mike's discoveries about John Batten are perhaps even more telling. When Mike finds Batten undressed in a motel room with a stenographer, he does not kill him to revenge his father's death, as he intended, but rather he recognizes him as a kind of double, another man lost in the world of lies; as Batten puts it, "Up to my ears in shit. . . . We all are. All we can do is whisper together, 'Don't make waves' " (222).

Thoroughly victimized by his own nature and that of the world of lies, Mike moves deeply into the darkness within himself as well as the racial darkness the attempted assassination has unleashed on the state. In the night of confusion and terror following the attempted assassination, he finds his father's lifelong family of servants hiding in the garage for fear of white violence. He had earlier spent a long night of carousing and fighting and brotherhood with his father's driver, Jay, whom he had known all his life, but whatever gains they might have made that night are lost in this one. Mike drives the family home to Black Bottom, feeling forever alienated from these people by the inescapable fact of race in a racist society: "Whatever his feelings were or would be he was wearing the uniform, the coloring of the enemy, by birth. It was like coming under a flag of truce into the enemy camp. The hush around him was tense and alien and hostile. He might even have been afraid or angry if he hadn't been so ashamed" (276). His shame and confusion lead him to travel to the birthplace of his father, to touch ground with the reality of his father, his life as well as his death. There, in the abandoned, paintless shack which is the tangible source of at least one half of his personal heritage, he finds an escaped convict with a knife. They struggle, and Mike disarms the convict, but decides not to turn him in, to do "nothing. . . . Nothing at all. I'm ready to call it quits." (280).

The existential freedom of this confrontation at the birthplace of his father, for all its desperation, prepares Mike finally to accept the wisdom of his mother, of the other half of his personal heritage. When she and her children are waiting to be driven to the Judge's funeral, she asks of them an honest recognition of the man in all his complexity:

In many ways a good and admirable man. But narrow too, and often vain and petty and even cruel, and crippled by pride long before some men crippled him with their fists. A hurt man. And all of us hurt him one way or another; all of us let ourselves be hurt by him. I ought to weep for him, to weep for us all, but the truth is it's too late for that now. Let us simply try to be a bit less foolish and to love one another (205).

51
THE FINISHED MAN

At the end of the novel Mike has not only begun to recognize the moral complexity of the world around him, but he has also recognized it in himself and not allowed that recognition to paralyze him. "When you break something," he tells L. J. Benjamin, Senator Parker's longtime associate and campaign manager who had resigned when Vivian Blanch gained the Senator's ear, "somebody's got to stoop over and start to pick up the pieces. I'm fixing to start trying to clean up a little behind myself." Benjamin, with a telling echo and reversal of Mike's despairing cry at his father's birthplace, "Nothing. . . . I'm ready to call it quits," replies, "That's better than nothing. . . . A whole lot better than nothing at all" (283). Mike has avoided remaining either a witness or a victim in Vivian Blanch's world in which all truth is nothing but appearance; he has accepted the duplicitous nature of reality and is willing both to take responsibility for it and to act to make it better. He has truly become the *finished* man of the title (which comes from and refers to William Butler Yeats's poem about the complexities of living in a real world, "A Dialogue of Self and Soul"), not a man who has finished with life and with living, but a man who has come through, who has grown up and can face living in the world of lies.

The religious ground of the novel becomes

clear not only in Mike's finally responding to his mother's wisdom, but also in the movement from the Old Testament world of Judge Royle, a world of heroism and judgment, to the New Testament world of Mike's new understanding, a world of forgiveness and love. The Judge seemed from another, more elemental and fundamental time; the descriptions in the "King of the Mountain" sequence make him seem larger than life: "his fists like hammers, his great bald head shining like a polished stone" (25), and (his self-description) "I got blood like hot turpentine in my veins and two big fists like knotty pine, like cypress knees, and I got a head like a cannon ball" (34). Even his wife compares him to "Samson pulling the roof down on the Philistines" (28). But for all his force and virtue, the Judge finally fails, just as, according to Christian theology, the Law failed, to be replaced by a new dispensation of personal redemption and mercy and the new law of love. The old order passes in *The Finished Man*, as it must, but it is transformed into something new; it is replaced and perhaps even superseded.

The election of John Batten is not itself without an element of real, if ironic, hope: "At least he was young enough to have youth's shine of possibility around him like a magic cloak, though already it must have seemed to him to have a mocking luster

THE FINISHED MAN

like the remnants of original fire that haunted the fallen angels" (278). And Mike's decision to defend the attempted assassin marks both a departure from his father's values and a fulfillment of them; when asked what he thinks the Judge would have thought, he states both his independence from and reconciliation with his father by saying: "I'm not asking myself that question, I'll make a fair guess, though. Under the circumstances I expect he might approve" (288). The novel ends with Mike's leaving the campaign headquarters "without looking back" and standing on the sidewalk, "waiting until his eyes got used to the hard bright light" (288).

In the "hard bright light" of reality one has no option in George Garrett's world but to face the light and the hard bright truth as well. In an open letter written in 1968 explaining why he did not have a poem for an anthology of poems honoring John F. Kennedy on the fifth anniversary of his assassination, Garrett described his initiation into working in a political campaign and into losing in the 1952 and 1956 Stevenson presidential campaigns:

The experience of working hard and long, of wishing and failing, the experience of *defeat* had an interesting effect on me. Instead of losing faith in the democratic process, I came along with more faith in it than when I had begun. . . . It seemed to me then that somehow we had lost touch with the needs and aspirations of the people, and that the people had told us that. . . we had to prove ourselves in defeat.[9]

Although Mike decides not to continue a career in politics, the attitude toward defeat expressed by Garrett in the letter is very much the one that leads Mike to offer to defend the young black man and not to opt out of his personal political responsibility. It is the same attitude that leads Garrett in the much darker context of "Main Currents of American Political Thought" to continue to *force* himself to vote, even if he fears that he may be only choosing among scoundrels.

The closing paragraph of that open letter also parallels the end of *The Finished Man* and offers as direct an expression of Garrett's Christian response to the question of moral behavior in a fallen world as he has ever made:

I test my own weakness and my charity to the quick by trying to love an unlovely world. Not for its ugliness, not in spite of it either. But because I am not the maker of it. And, in truth, I have not been asked whether I want to expend my love upon it. I have been *told* to. Of course, theologically this is a Commandment, but I believe it is also a "description of reality," to hate is to die, to love is to live.[10]

THE FINISHED MAN

Using the traditional techniques of realistic fiction, strongly influenced by Warren and Faulkner, *The Finished Man* is nevertheless a strong first step toward the complexities of Garrett's later fiction, and it is, in its own right, a distinctive and strongly personal statement by its author. The world of *The Finished Man* is one which, when exposed to the hard bright light of the committed imagination, reveals itself in all of its corruption and violence, betrayal and duplicity. It is the ambiguously free world described in the concluding sentence of "The Seacoast of Bohemia," one in which "Nothing, good or evil, is impossible any more."[11] Nevertheless, it is one in which we have no choice but to live and to "try to be a little bit less foolish and to love one another."

Notes

1. *The Collected Poems of George Garrett* (Fayetteville: University of Arkansas Press, 1984) 9.

2. John Graham and W. R. Robinson, "George Garrett Discusses Writing and His Work," *Mill Mountain Review* 1 (1971): 85.

3. George Garrett, *The Finished Man* (New York: Scribner's, 1959) 15. Further references will be noted parenthetically.

4. Graham and Robinson 85.

5. Graham and Robinson 84.

6. Garrett, *An Evening Performance* (Garden City: Doubleday,

1985) 17. Further references to the short story "King of the Mountain" are to this edition and will be noted parenthetically.

7. Garrett, *King of the Mountain* (New York: Scribner's, 1957) 94.

8. W. R. Robinson, "Imagining the Individual: George Garrett's *Death of the Fox*," *The Hollins Critic* 8 (1971): 8.

9. "An Open Letter from George Garrett," 9 ed. *toward winter* Harry Nash and Robert Bonazzi (Houston: Latitudes Press, 1968) [35–37]. I have regularized the editors' eccentric capitalization and punctuation.

10. Nash and Bonazzi [49].

11. Garrett, *King of the Mountain* 74.

CHAPTER THREE

Which Ones Are the Enemy?

George Garrett chose to end his first collection of short stories, *King of the Mountain*, with a sequence of five army stories gathered under the collective title "What's the Purpose of the Bayonet?" The last of these, "Torment," closes the book with a hellish vision of life as it unavoidably is. The narrator had thrilled as a pubescent child to an illustration in *The History of the World* (the best "pornographic" material to which he had access) called "The Inquisition in Session":

It showed a full-blown woman as naked as God made her, hiding her face. A huge executioner with a black mask on had just ripped away the last shreds of her clothes. In the background there was a raised bench with ecclesiastical dignitaries, bored or leering, and in one corner there were instruments of torture, whips and irons heating red-hot on a fire. It was a perfect field-day for undeveloped sexuality. An innocent's paradise."[1]

Later, when he is a soldier in Linz, Austria, he witnesses at the main police station a roundup of the town's whores. Since there were no severe penalties for prostitution, the police, in a vain effort to scare the women, beat them horribly and bloodily: "It was like a picture out of Dante's *Inferno*" (45). The narrative concludes:

> I was sick thinking about the fine avenues and boulevards of this world where you walk with your head up, strut if you want to like a god, and meanwhile all the time there's an invisible world breeding and thriving. In back rooms, in hidden corners, behind blank smiles, all over the world people are suffering and making other people suffer. The things God has to see because He cannot shut His eyes! It's almost too much to think about. It's enough to turn your stomach against the whole inhuman race (46).

The "innocent's paradise," the masturbatory teenager's delight of bloodless sexual violence, proves to be a false paradise from which one must necessarily fall into hellish reality if one is ever really to grow up, to gain any sort of adult moral victory in the awful presence of that "invisible world."

Like the army novels of James Jones, Garrett's army fiction takes place within the context of the "invisible world" of suffering, and the army—with

WHICH ONES ARE THE ENEMY?

its system of rigorously controlled order which exists only because of a larger disorder—offers him a powerful metaphoric structure with which to deal with the fallen world of lies at its worst. *Which Ones Are the Enemy?*, Garrett's second novel, stands as the powerful centerpiece of a cluster of short stories: "Don't Take No for an Answer," "How the Last War Ended," "The Blood of Strangers," and "What's the Purpose of the Bayonet?" from *King of the Mountain;* and "The Old Army Game," "The Wounded Soldier," "Unmapped Country," and "Texarkana Was a Crazy Town" from *Cold Ground Was My Bed Last Night*. Each of these works opens a window on that "invisible world," with the rules and regulations of the army as a system of artificially imposed coordinates by which the reader is able to comprehend fully the chaos of that terrible reality.

The narrator of "Texarkana Was a Crazy Town," a very competent soldier, a chief-of-section in the artillery, leaves the army (in which he had enlisted when he was seventeen) despite the warnings of his best friend, a black sergeant named Mooney, who tells him: "You've got it made here. You don't know it. You just don't know how it is. You don't know anything else but the army. It's going to be tough out there for a guy like you, believe me" (288). The young soldier goes back into civilian life only to find a chaos of sexual sickness, racial hatred, and pointless violence which sickens him: "I felt so sick about everything in the whole world I wanted to die. I just wanted to fall over dead" (301). And worse, he discovers in himself the same qualities he had found in the world; during a fight in which he wants to kill his opponent, "to tear him into pieces and stamp them in the dust," he realizes what he is doing: "I knew what had happened to me and I knew I wasn't a damn bit better than those guys that beat up Peanuts or Delma or Pete or anybody else. I was so sick of myself I felt like I was going to puke" (302).

Unable to deal with the disorder he has discovered in the world and in himself, he turns from the freedom and responsibility of civilian life and flees back to the army, to his old outfit, to Mooney's room. The order he finds there brings him the peace he has been seeking:

He wasn't there but the room had his touch on everything in it. It was bare and clean and neat. The clothes in his wall locker were hanging evenly. The boots under his bed, side by side, were shined up nice, not all spit-shined like some young soldier's, just a nice shine. I made up the empty bunk. I made it up real tight without a wrinkle, so tight you could bounce a quarter off of it if you wanted to. Then I threw all my stuff in the corner and just flopped down in the

WHICH ONES ARE THE ENEMY?

middle of my bunk. I felt like I was floating on top of water (303).

The army, for all the ironies of the situation, gives this young soldier a home, a friend, a monastic retreat from the moral chaos of life with which he cannot deal, but few of Garrett's other soldiers can escape so easily. Their lives and woes and genuine suffering are, as the narrator of "The Old Army Game" puts it, "small doings, negligible discomforts. It would be sheer sentimentality to claim otherwise. And I'm not cockeyed enough to think that such events could arouse Pity and Terror. Nothing of Great Men Falling from High Place in our time. A battle royal in the anthill maybe. No, the simple facts, arranged and related . . . will never do that. But they are nevertheless not insignificant" (213). To explain himself, the narrator goes on to quote a passage from Maxim Gorky's novel *Bystander* which may stand as a rationale for all of Garrett's army fiction, both its matter and its manner:

Why do I relate these abominations? So that you may know, kind sirs, that all is not past and done with! You have a liking for grim fantasies; you are delighted by horrible stories well told; the grotesquely terrible excites you pleasantly. But I know of genuine horrors, everyday terrors, and I have the undeniable right to

UNDERSTANDING GEORGE GARRETT

excite you unpleasantly by telling you about them, in order that you may remember how we live, and under what circumstances. A low and unclean life it is, ours, and that is the truth.

I am a lover of humanity, and I have no desire to make anyone miserable, but one must not be sentimental, nor hide the grim truth with the motley words of beautiful lies. Let us face life as it is! All that is good and human in our hearts needs renewing (213).

The substance and texture of Garrett's army stories is that of "grim truth," of "life as it is" without the "motley words of beautiful lies." Those lies are, of course, not the "beautiful lie" of a parable which contains the truth, for these stories are parabolic, but rather the lies a complacent society tells itself in order to keep the world of suffering out of sight and out of mind, to keep it "invisible." The army stories are told from within, often in first person, told by participants and not by observers, actors and not witnesses, sinners and not saints; and yet by the very act of telling, of not looking away, the truth reveals itself and redemption becomes possible. They are certainly "not insignificant."

Which Ones Are the Enemy? is the story of, and is told by, a soldier, Private John Riche, "just plain Riche, like in son-of-a-bitch."[2] Riche is, by his own account, a born loser: "They ought to have a rib-

WHICH ONES ARE THE ENEMY?

bon and a medal for guys like me—a Congressional Medal for Losers. You could wear a ribbon around your neck, and instead of saluting you people could give you a high sign with the middle finger" (3). The story he tells in the novel is of the one time "I almost fooled myself that I was breaking the mold. . . . And I came close to kidding myself right out of the habit of losing" (3). It is, as Garrett noted, "a very small and rather sordid episode which probably didn't take more than a couple of pages in the file in the Trieste command somewhere."[3] But it is the major event in John Riche's life, a moment of significant truth in the world of lies or, as Riche would put it, the world of "phoniness."

The events of the novel take place in the early 1950s in the Free Territory of Trieste, where the occupying American troops were in the command ironically named TRUST—Trieste United States Troops. The morally free territory of the novel is a rocky wasteland at Opicina near the Yugoslavian border, "as far out of it as possible" (19):

Rocks, that's the first thing I saw, the shine and sparkle of sunlight on rocks. Rocks everywhere, more rocks than I had ever seen before in one place except in a quarry or a graveyard. There were small cleared fields for farming, with high walls of picked up rocks around them. And there were a few stunted pine trees, all twisted and gnarled from fighting for life and juice among the rocks, and it looked like they had suffered plenty from wind too. . . . Just try and imagine farming land like that? . . . It would wring the last ounce of sweat out of you in one lifetime, and you would probably end up sitting with your face in the sun, nothing but a dry, rattling husk, like a cured gourd of skin and bones (6–7).

Riche, a dweller in a spiritual wasteland of his own, decides that "the country and I deserved each other" and that "if God Himself had wanted to find the right spot to assign me to, He couldn't have done any better" (7).

John Riche is a professional soldier, a man who lives in this wasteland by choice. He has experienced both a kind of desperate existential freedom and an almost tunnel-vision view of the impersonal truth of things:

Every bullet and shell fragment is postmarked To Whom It May Concern. Even God shrugs His shoulders and you got to take your own chances. . . . Now knowing that may be tough to take too. I mean nobody, not God, not the enemy whoever they may be, or even your own guys, is really interested in *you*. And, of course, all you're interested in is yourself. It's scary, but once you get used to the idea it's not so bad. You are kind of free in a wild, breathless way. . . . You're free of responsibility if not

WHICH ONES ARE THE ENEMY?

worry. You get where one pair of dry socks is the most important thing in the whole universe. . . . And—who knows?—maybe that's the whole truth, in combat or out of it. Maybe one pair of dry socks is the most sense one man all alone can ever make out of any of it (68).

John Riche has applied his combat truth to the whole of his life. Ernest Hemingway's Harry Morgan, another character living in a moral wasteland, spends all his life learning that "no matter how a man alone ain't got no bloody fucking chance."[4] Riche's combat wisdom teaches him that "one man all alone" has got a chance, "in combat or out of it," if he hangs on to his one pair of dry socks, if he soldiers carefully and well, if he doesn't take adversity (or anything else) personally, and if he takes care of himself, remains interested only in himself, and stays "free of responsibility."

Upon this limited view of "the whole truth," Riche has constructed a darkly stoic philosophy of action, the central premise of which is: "I can't afford to have too many things I can't do without" (84). Jack Wright Rhodes has called Riche's code of behavior "the art of noninvolvement," and he goes on to suggest that Riche "realizes that caring means vulnerability," and that "he has no trouble staying uninvolved through much of the novel because of the phoniness he sees surrounding him."[5]

UNDERSTANDING GEORGE GARRETT

Riche's stoic "art of noninvolvement" allows him the illusion of detachment, of being able to stand aside and judge the behavior around him. Upon his arrival at the *caserma* (barracks) of the Nth Field Artillery, he insists on the rules and demands that the driver of the truck unhook the safety strap and let down the tail-gate before he will get off because *"It's the responsibility of the driver"* (6); he assigns responsibility within the parameters of any given job, and he expects everyone, including himself, to fulfill that specific responsibility. But he allows himself to remain free of the larger responsibility of caring for others, of being responsible for others, of exercising Christian charity.

Riche respects people who know their jobs and who do them to the letter, and he despises "phoniness" with the intensity of Holden Caulfield in J. D. Salinger's *The Catcher in the Rye*. In fact, as Kenneth Hamilton has noted, "The word 'phony' has become so associated with Holden that it now carries the overtones of his use of it," his application of it "to the false values of the materialistic adult world, with its unrestrained egotism and consequent double standards, subterfuges, venality, and violence."[6] John Riche is, as Garrett's insistence on the word "phony" indicates, a kind of hard-boiled Holden Caulfield, who knows that "caring means vulnerability" and who

WHICH ONES ARE THE ENEMY?

fools himself and evades the truth about himself and his relationship to others in a tough, real world where games are played for keeps and there is no innocent little sister to whom to turn for salvation in the end. Riche, according to Garrett, "is, in part, an unsuccessful con man" who is "allowed to make his own case, to con the reader a little bit"; but, as is the case with any first-person narrator, "if he can fool you, he can fool himself too."[7] Like Holden Caulfield, John Riche thinks he can live apart from his fellow human beings behind a shield of noninvolvement. But where Holden meets Phoebe and rediscovers through her innocence the existence of a "nice" world, Riche meets Angela and discovers through her genuineness and her suffering both his own capacity for caring and the awful truth that "these are the times of Jeremiah and Isaiah and Job" (152).

Sergeant Jethroe, Riche's "roommate," a war-ravaged soldier "on the bumpy, deep-rutted, well-traveled road to Loonyville" (67), underlines the appropriateness of Old Testament prophecy to life in TRUST by regularly writing passages from the Bible on pieces of paper and giving them to Riche. The first of these, Isaiah 59:9, which Riche still keeps "in my wallet to this day for some reason," defines the moral wasteland in which the events of the novel take place: "Therefore is judgment far

UNDERSTANDING GEORGE GARRETT

from us, and justice shall not overtake us. We looked for light, and behold darkness; brightness, and we have walked in the dark" (72). The last of Jethroe's notes, Job 17:14, helps Riche to define himself in the depth of his loss at the end of the novel: "I have said to corruption, Thou art my father: to the worm, Thou art my mother, and my sister" (209). For Riche to be able to understand what Jethroe sees in his madness and his belief, he must first undergo the experience of learning to love another and the crushing defeat of losing the one he has learned to love; the force of the experience not only allows him self-discovery, but it also gives him the ability to articulate what he has discovered and is discovering. Beyond a sense of fate, of a vaguely defined "They" who function as Nemesis in the phony world through which he moves, Riche has only his narrow combat truth to use as a ground for understanding. It is through his relationship with Angela (with the undertone of Jethroe's reiteration of prophetic utterance) that he is able to restate his combat truth, to give it an intensity and larger meaning beyond its focus on the self:

In Basic Training the old sergeants used to say: "Give your soul to God because your ass is mine." That's the way it was. In certain situations, some very tight spot

WHICH ONES ARE THE ENEMY?

or corner, you can give your soul to God all right. And then, with that out of the way and all taken care of, you can bear down, concentrate on nothing else but what you are doing. And it's a kind of a clean, crazy joy. If you live through a time like that They sometimes give you a medal for it. But that medal doesn't mean a thing. Because if you really gave your soul to God you can't ever get it back again. Even if you want it back. That's the way I felt. That's the way I feel (125).

Riche knows that "women have always been a special weakness of mine and they have pretty near always led me the straightest and shortest route to trouble" (84); but Angela, a B-girl at the Kit Kat Club in Trieste, attracts him because of a glimpse of genuineness he sees when she does not know anyone is looking, a sadness which she covers immediately with the smile and charm of "a devilish creature of joy straight out of a lazy sex dream. . . . I think it was seeing her both ways like that, true and false, that really grabbed me" (86). Riche resents the way Angela needles him about being short, and he is further challenged by *her* noninvolvement, *her* refusal to care. As she puts it: "If I am with one man I'm true to him. . . . I do everything the right way. But there is one thing I do not do. I don't *care*. I never care. Nobody can ever make me care" (39). He accepts the challenge and decides to pay her back for hurting his feelings, to "pay the whole world back through her" (104). He decides not only to get her to shack up with him, but to make her care, to make her think she loves him:

> I knew it could be done from hard experience. She might be tough all right, but somewhere she would be brittle enough to break down and fall down in little pieces. Like an idol to worship and a victim to sacrifice at the same time. Like a shrine and a latrine in the same place. Like the strange gods old King Solomon fell down and worshiped when he just couldn't stand himself or even the thought of God any more. And they say King Solomon was a wise man. Wiser than most before or since. Still, wise or not, he had to go down and chew the bitter grass and howl like all the rest of us (104).

Riche succeeds in making Angela care, but in doing so, no wiser than Solomon, he begins to care for Angela:

> The thing is that neither one of us had wanted to care. That was about the last thing that either one of us had wanted. She had known all along, whatever I did good or bad with her, that I was just playing the part. Of course as a shack job she had her part to play too. So she didn't blame me for that and she didn't let it worry her. After all, she said, there were times when it seemed like a pretty good part to play. And then we both knew what we had really known all along. That

WHICH ONES ARE THE ENEMY?

maybe that's all there is to it between two people—
playing your part. That maybe it's all a man can hope
for. It would be hard to say if one part was more *true*
or *real* than another one. Brave man or coward, wise
man or fool, saint or sinner. The thing to do, then,
was to act with care, because if you play long enough
you may become the part you are playing (120).

Playing their parts as lovers, they begin to share their lives together, their pasts as well as the present. Angela tells Riche her story—of the war, of her German lover and husband, of her punishment as a collaborator, of her baby Wilhelm whom she gave away and who has no memory of her, of her American lover and the venereal disease he gave her, of the American's baby girl who was born blind and whom she also gave away, of her hopeless poverty and being driven into prostitution, of her desperate journey to find her German husband, whom she finds crippled after a stay in a Russian prison camp and who has remarried, and of her equally desperate return to Trieste and to Opicina. As he listens to her story, Riche both recognizes it as "true and typical, . . . a very common story these days" and empathizes with her completely, "as if it *had* happened to me" (153).

Riche talks to Angela of his life, too, "slowly, like a sick man clearing his throat to spit out his insides" (121)—the story of "a born loser, but a loser with big ideas, who found a home and an asylum among the other losers of the U.S. Army" (121). He tells her the important things of his life, even his experiences in Korea—things he never talked to his army buddies about because they took so much for granted, the shared experience of "fear, dirt, hot and dry, wet and cold, hungry, the death of friends and enemies. The simple things of the trade of soldiering" (122). For the first time in his life he articulates and begins to understand the complex truths of his life beyond his stoical combat truth: "The truth is I had never put any of it together in my mind because I had never had to. I had never tried to tell a soul, not even myself, about it in words. I had never tried to make any sense out of it" (122). This coming to terms with his experience in the act of intimate speech is what will ultimately allow Riche to tell his story in the novel, in the "conversation that goes on in an unbroken way between the reader and the writer."

Riche and Angela build a bond of love between themselves, "share themselves, . . . take their separate selves and their pasts and mingle them together," and "speak to each other about these things in words without having to tell lies" (158). They have both "had all the big jokes played on us," and they have the ability, together, to laugh

WHICH ONES ARE THE ENEMY?

and to love. Riche says that it was "like we were dancing . . . in step and in tune with everything under the sun" (158). But then he sums up their full and open relationship more simply: "Better to say it was good and simple. Better to say that once we were able to shuck off our disguises and costumes as simply as shucking off our clothes we had lost a heavy weight. We felt lighthearted and able to rejoice" (158).

Angela and John Riche find an oasis of love in the desert in which they both have lived for so long, but the love which they share also makes them hostage to each other's fate. They have learned to care and have come alive, but they have also become vulnerable, no longer armored in indifference. In order to have the money, first to win (and win over) Angela, and then to share a real life with her, Riche has joined in a black-market scheme with a fellow soldier, Corporal Stitch, "a kind of small-time operator" (73) who figures in an earlier Garrett short story, "Don't Take No for an Answer." In that story Stitch behaves as an almost mirror opposite to Riche in his treatment of a woman, a homely American schoolteacher whom he cons into an affair while he is on leave in Paris. He uses her and leaves her, and later he sums up the affair for his fellow soldiers: "You keep telling a pig she's wonderful and they start believing it. Hell, I almost believed it. By the end of the time I almost started to like the bitch" (91). Stitch is what Riche thought he was before his feelings for Angela led him to examine his life, so in a sense Riche has formed a partnership with his former self, the selfish operator who does not care. The results are disastrous.

Riche promises Angela he will get out of the black market; if he is caught, she tells him, "I'd die. . . . I'd want to be dead. . . . I don't want anything to hurt you again" (125). By the time Riche does get caught, Angela is pregnant with his child. They have no hope of getting married, because they are both snared in finished but still legally binding marriages. His arrest ends what hope they have of even being together, especially when Stitch panics, kills a policeman, and is killed himself, and the army decides to break up the Nth Field, which is giving the command a bad name. Angela, in despair, kills herself with a pistol that Riche had given her, taught her how to use, and given her the depth of feeling for another person that drives her to use it.

Riche finds himself alone in the wasteland again, in an absurd world like the one he once saw in Korea in an observation post when "we didn't know what was going on, and we couldn't tell one

WHICH ONES ARE THE ENEMY?

side from the other" (123). The forward observer who hadn't slept for days kept stalling on the calling down of fire missions until he finally cracked and yelled in anger and fear to Riche, "Which ones are the enemy? . . . Jesus Christ. . . . Which ones are the freaking enemy?" (124).

Love does not survive in the wasteland, but it is the only thing that makes the wasteland habitable. John Riche does survive; like Frederic Henry in Hemingway's *A Farewell to Arms,* he lives to tell the tale and even finds a final victory of sorts in that telling.

Like Henry, Riche visits the corpse of his lover; but unlike Henry, who finds it to be "like saying good-by to a statue," he lets his "heart crack and break to pieces" (208). The love he had and has for Angela is so strong that it still holds true; he remembers "how that sweet flesh had lived once" (208), and, looking at her toes, he laughs "because her toes were funny and unbeautiful and she had always been shy and ashamed of them. And I loved them more than all the parts of myself put together" (209). The two Italian morgue attendants glare at him with hatred, but he assures the reader that "I swear to God it was an honest laugh. And the best prayer I could leave her with" (209).

He does not explain to the Italians, and he brutally rejects the sympathy of his MP guards, not allowing them to "have a nickel's worth of cheap, phony feelings" (210). He guards himself against their phoniness by pretending callous indifference, by bumming a cigarette for the ride back to his cell:

I was thinking that as long as I could keep on smoking and concentrating on nothing else but the pleasure of it, I wouldn't have to cry in front of them. Even if I did, though, even if I let go and couldn't help myself, the wind blowing in my face would dry my tears so fast no one would ever notice it (211).

Riche conceals his true feelings from his guards, particularly a young college boy MP, as a reaction against their phony sympathy which demands that he behave a certain way; as he says, "Let him live and learn like the rest of us. Let him earn his own lumps" (210). His actions and his statement parallel in their own parabolic way Christ's explanation to the disciples of why he teaches in parables: "That seeing they may see, and not perceive; and hearing they may hear, and not understand; lest at any time they should be converted, and their sins should be forgiven them" (Mark 4:12). Riche is no savior, but he has learned that true empathy and true understanding must be earned, and that phony sympathy is just another lie in a world of lies; each one of us must "live and learn like the rest of us."

WHICH ONES ARE THE ENEMY?

He conceals the truth from those around him who shouldn't hear, who are too quick to judge and too quick to sentimentalize. He is still, however, the man who loved and learned with Angela, and he is no longer exempt from caring; he has learned to articulate his experience, and he offers it in the form of the novel to those who are willing to listen to the whole truth, to the story told from the inside. "Don't ask me why," he begins his story. "Never ask me why" (3). He does not *explain* the truth, but he does *express* it, he does *share* it with an openness he learned from his time with Angela. He has long since given his soul irrevocably to God, but he is not yet ready to ask God for anything more than forgiveness for Angela, for her suicide: "Me? I wasn't asking Him for any favors. We'll come to that by and by" (208). But he is ready to tell the tale, to learn and to share by that telling, with the double understanding that it is almost impossible to know which ones are the enemy and that all that is good and human in our hearts does need renewing. Garrett's use of the first-person narrative voice, letting Riche directly address his readers, allows Riche the consolation of his confession and permits his readers to live and learn along with him: to experience life as it is in the too often "invisible" world with its genuine horrors and everyday terrors; to know what it is "to keep on standing up and asking for more (more *what?* well, trouble maybe) until I'm *really* out, horizontal, heels up, white-eyed" (3).

The reader's act of communion with this born loser is the central point and key to this novel's real and significant value, to its distinctive identity.

Notes

1. George Garrett, *An Evening Performance* (Garden City: Doubleday, 1985) 44. Further references to short fiction will be to this edition unless otherwise noted and will be noted parenthetically.

2. Garrett, *Which Ones Are the Enemy?* (Boston: Little, Brown, 1961) 13. Further references will be noted parenthetically.

3. John Graham and W. R. Robinson, "George Garrett Discusses Writing and His Work," *Mill Mountain Review* 1 (1971): 87.

4. Ernest Hemingway, *To Have and Have Not* (New York: Scribner's, 1937) 225.

5. Jack Wright Rhodes, "George Garrett," *Vol. 2 of American Novelists Since World War II. Dictionary of Literary Biography;* ed. Jeffrey Helterman and Richard Layman (Detroit: Bruccoli Clark / Gale, 1978) 187.

6. Kenneth Hamilton, *J. D. Salinger* (Grand Rapids: Eerdmans, 1967) 22.

7. Graham and Robinson 87, 86.

CHAPTER FOUR

Do, Lord, Remember Me

Do, Lord, Remember Me is one of the richest, most complex, and rewarding of George Garrett's novels and, because of the history of its publication, perhaps the most frustrating and tantalizing. Published first in Great Britain and then later the same year in the United States, the novel as it stands represents only about a fourth of the manuscript of the novel as Garrett originally wrote it; there are numerous differences between the two published versions of the text as well, with the British version being the fuller and the more sexually explicit of the two. The complete and unpublished novel had to do with the characters clustered around Red Smalley, the traveling evangelist who arrives in the small town of High Pines, North Carolina, and with the lives of the people in the town as they are affected by that visit. But when the pressures of publication required radical cutting, Garrett removed almost all of the material concerning the townspeople, leaving the novel focused sharply on the evangelist and his entourage.

In addition to the differences between the two published versions of the novel, other fragments of the original manuscript which were reshaped by Garrett into separate short novels offer some evidence of the kind of book the novel would have been. In 1964, the short novel "Cold Ground Was My Bed Last Night"—which was retitled "Noise of Strangers" for its appearances in *The Magic Striptease* and *An Evening Performance*—was published as the title story in a collection of Garrett's short fiction. This piece, Garrett has said, was originally conceived as part of the novel: "Once upon a time that story was conceived of in my mind as a kind of curtain-raiser for this story; they were going to be together."[1] The material concerning the townspeople Garrett hoped "to use . . . in another way," perhaps in "a sequel of sorts"; and two differing versions of a short novel which does function as "a sequel of sorts" to *Do, Lord, Remember Me* have been published: "To Whom Shall I Turn Now in My Hour of Need"—in *A Wreath for Garibaldi*—and the longer, more complex "The Satyr Shall Cry," which first appeared in *The Magic Striptease*. Both versions of this short novel function as a grotesque fun-house mirror image of *Do, Lord, Remember Me*,

DO, LORD, REMEMBER ME

presenting an absurd vision of the town as a microcosm of the larger world of human vice and folly, giving a richly comic context worthy of a Chaucer or a Fielding (two of Garrett's professed literary masters) to the intense spiritual parable of the novel.

A reader, then, who wishes to understand this powerful novel fully must not only come to terms with it as a separate entity, but also must be aware of its satellite short novels—the "curtain-raiser" and the darkly comic mirror image—both of which do exert a gravitational pull on the larger work.

"Noise of Strangers" concerns Jack Riddle, the sheriff of Fairview, a small Florida town, "a preserved relic, it seems, of what at least from this anxious point in human history was an easier, gentler, more relaxed time to be alive,"[2] an oasis of shade and civilization in the midst of "the shadeless glare that leaps toward a vague horizon" (472); the sheriff's ambitious young deputy, Larry Berlin; and Ike Toombs, a vagrant who has been arrested after a shoot-out between Berlin and the man in whose car Toombs claims to have been hitching a ride. The deputy's killing the driver and taking Toombs into custody brings into the town, according to Garrett, "alien and very dangerous forces."[3] These forces thrust the sheriff (and thereby the town) out of the peaceful shade of moral security and into the "shadeless glare" of the morally ambiguous world of lies, into this "anxious point in human history."

The sheriff, who conceives of his role "as beyond the simple boundaries of good and bad" because "he is not even sure what these words mean any more" (481), has determined to maintain the surface order of life in the town:

The Sheriff is, among other things, the chosen protector of his little world, the elected hero who must go forth to battle dragons and dark knights for them all while the townspeople live quiet and secure in the vague shine of the hidden treasure—respectability. He sees himself as a lone sentry protecting the chaste virtue of those fine houses along the main street. Within may be madness, despair, rage, and the seven deadly sins guarding a captive princess, but he is concerned only with the public world (482).

He has even come to terms with old pagan nature, keeping it under control (in the person of the town drunk, the Goatman) with a sort of benign despotism, keeping the Goatman around as a kind of emblem of "respectability turned inside out" (482), a tame warning to the town.

The explosion of violence into the town and the presence of the morally ambiguous wanderer, Ike Toombs, along with the new challenge to his

DO, LORD, REMEMBER ME

authority posed by the cockiness of his deputy after the killing, drain Riddle of both his legal authority and personal sense of power. The disorder represented by Toombs, who may or may not have been a partner of the dead driver in an armed robbery the night before, coupled with the almost fascistic quick-draw "order" of the aptly named deputy, Larry Berlin, push the sheriff beyond the role he has so long chosen to play. As Toombs notices, "There is something about the Sheriff's smile that is like the smile of a man who has tasted something evil and found that it is sweet and good to eat. The Sheriff is a different man" (504). He takes away the one possession (his guitar) that Ike Toombs values in the world for no other reason than he knows that Toombs represents to him: "Scum! Fungus on the tired face of the earth! They breed like maggots, feeding on dead things. Bounce aimless across the country landing one place and another like grasshoppers. A plague of grasshoppers! Might just as well have never been born" (512). Like a modern-day Pilate, the sheriff can only respond to Toombs's fear that he'll be killed for something he didn't do by saying, "It's out of my hands" (513). And he straps on, for the first time in his life, a gun, a symbol of his awareness, according to Garrett, that "he needed extra power."[4]

UNDERSTANDING GEORGE GARRETT

Ike Toombs has brought into the sheriff's life the things he does not want to see: his own hate, his own fallibility, his own weakness, the reality of evil even in Fairview. He can free the Goatman because he believes that the Goatman "can't help himself" (513) just as he can free a trapped fly out his office window, but he cannot free himself from the truth that Toombs has brought him anymore than he can avoid the challenge to his job posed by the young deputy, who has no intentions of remaining "in the shadow of Jack Riddle forever" (515). "Slowly, veil by veil, the truth has been revealed to him whether he wanted it that way or not," and he can no longer be "the protector of illusion, guardian of the secret nakedness. High priest of a veiled goddess. Obedient servant of the little, flimsy illusions of respectability and decency the townspeople live by and for" (507). As it did to Pilate, who asked "What is truth?" the truth has burst in upon him. Feeling "like an old man" (517), Sheriff Riddle must now face the riddle of himself as well as of the life around him; he can no longer serve the "veiled goddess" but must, like Garrett's other fallen characters who have seen the naked truth (Mike Royle and John Riche and the ones to follow), face the hard bright light and make his way in the world of lies. As the epigraph to the first appearance of the story (from Wallace

DO, LORD, REMEMBER ME

Stevens's "No Possum, No Sop, No Taters") suggests, "It is here, in this bad, that we reach / The last purity of the knowledge of good."[5]

In order to engage the reader in the moral complexities and ambiguities of "Noise of Strangers," Garrett shifts the restricted point of view from one to the other among Sheriff Riddle, Larry Berlin, and Ike Toombs. For the even more ambitious and ambiguous text of *Do, Lord, Remember Me*, he moves to a complex structure of shifting first-person points of view, a narrative device which also permits interior monologues from even deeper in the consciousness of the character. Garrett has said that "the construction of the book is what might be called an interrelated group of dramatic monologues. Each of the characters speaks almost directly to the reader in his own voice about what's happening."[6] Certainly the narrative technique will bring to mind William Faulkner's *As I Lay Dying*, but Garrett's narrative moves at a much faster pace, its style varying wildly from character to character, the eight narrators speaking in direct monologues that will suddenly open inward and become intensely real beyond the surfaces of either the events they are describing or even their conscious perceptions of those events.

No one character speaks the whole truth, nor do they all speak it by any simple process of addition, for they often contradict one another, see what they want to see, remember only what they dare to remember. Ike Toombs, in "Noise of Strangers," remembers how he spent the night of the robbery alone with only the cold ground as his bed, but the reader cannot know whether this "memory" is the product of true experience or desperate desire. In *Do, Lord, Remember Me* that kind of ambiguity is essential to the book's design, for the reader must not and cannot remain passive, but must become an active participant in the "copulative spirit" of the reading experience, in the creation of the truth of the novel. That truth is beyond bare statement; it is rather the very movement of things, the shape events take in the reader's mind, a frenzied comic dance of pain and folly which makes little sense to the dancers but, from the shared perspective of artistic vision, takes on real meaning, just as the circling passage of life's journey in time was said by medieval theologians to take on form and meaning at the center of the circle, the still point of eternity from which the whole can be seen and understood.

That Garrett's experimental and very modern narrative technique should be analogous to a medieval metaphor for the relationship of limited human and unlimited divine understanding is particularly apt for this novel, which is thoroughly

DO, LORD, REMEMBER ME

Chaucerian in conception and manner. The dedicatory epigraphs to both the British and American editions are taken from *The Canterbury Tales*, the former from Chaucer's "Retracciouns," in which he confesses that all that the reader might find to like in the work is from "oure Lord Jhesu Crist, of whom procedeth al wit and al goodnesse" and that all that displeases him must be attributed "to the defaute of myn unkonnynge, and nat to my wyl,"[7] and the latter from the prologue to "The Parson's Tale," in which the parson, "a Southren man," promises "a mery tale in prose / To knitte all this feeste, and make an ende"[8] (before proceeding to deliver a treatise upon the proper preparation for confession and the true nature of the seven deadly sins). Both epigraphs are appropriate; they indicate that the novel is a sincerely Christian work and also that this tragicomic novel is double-natured, "a mery tale" which is composed of a series of inner confessions and one which deals seriously and directly with the deadliness of sin.

The South of *Do, Lord, Remember Me* is, like Chaucer's England, a confused landscape in which religion and sex, honesty and petty evil, the haunting dream of purity and the fallen world of lies are so subtly interwoven that no one can judge another or even himself or herself, and in which the most serious of religious pilgrimages is at once an occasion for true religious feeling and unrestrained bawdiness. Garrett's characters, like Chaucer's, are types, bigger than life, caricatures and symbols, but also, like the Canterbury pilgrims, alive with a realistic color and freshness that sticks and grows bright in the mind. And, of course, Garrett, like Chaucer, is a Christian artist whose parables convey the truth of the spirit while fully expressing the failings of the flesh and the strivings of the soul.

In Garrett's poem "Revival" the speaker describes the exaggerated and grotesquely ambivalent quality of the world of a tent revivalist, in which "chaos has pitched a tent / in my pasture" with "Fire and brimstone, thunder and lightning, / telegrams in the unknown tongue," and "The bushes . . . crawling with couples," but leaving finally

> Nothing
> to prove they camped here and tried
> to raise a crop of hell except
> that scar of dead space (where the tent was)
> like a huge footprint.

The ambiguities and ironies in the poem are compound, and Garrett makes them explicit by comparing the evangelist's world to that of the mythic giants "of the morning world," into whose domain

DO, LORD, REMEMBER ME

> Came then Christ
> to climb the thorny beanstalk
> and save us one and all.⁹

Another parallel poem, "Holy Roller," expands the portrait of the traveling evangelist and adds to it the concept of the sinner who is chosen, who by the unimaginable strangeness of God's grace is made both a victim and an instrument of God's love and human salvation. In the poem Garrett describes the evangelist, whose interests and successes are as sexual as they are religious; whose "whiteness" troubles "young virgins where they kneel" and whose "dark and hoarse" voice "tickles the goodwives where they live." His sinfulness like the devil himself is open for all to know ("On, I know you of old, brother"), but, Garrett continues:

> I know this too:
> the ways of God are crazy, daze
> a skeptic mind like summer lightning.
> Others false and foolish as you (and I)
> have been chosen and, so chosen,
> babbled more wisely than they knew.
> You bow your handsome goathead and
> God springs from your lips like a snowy dove (18).

This enigmatic and charismatic figure, "false and foolish as you (and I)" and yet chosen to bear the necessary burden of God's word, is, in the person of Big Red Smalley, at the center of *Do, Lord, Remember Me*, of a modern Christian parable of man's endless and painful folly in the mad and fallen world of lies.

The plot of the novel, for all its complications, has the final simplicity of good parable; it does, as the epigraph from "The Parson's Tale" suggests, "make an ende," the end of a pilgrimage, the end of Red Smalley's revival show, and the end of his life. The novel takes place during the time of a full moon in the short span of hours in which Smalley arrives in High Pines; makes the arrangements for his show; preaches his final sermon, during which he is possessed by God and throws all the money made over the course of a long tour to the congregation; and finds his own death even as the other characters find their own separate kinds of peace.

Smalley is at the center of the story, and he dominates those around him with the power of his personality. He has a criminal past and another name (L. J. Griggs), for, like St. Paul, he was overtaken by the power and shed his former self like a snake's discarded skin. Perhaps more like that serpent than St. Paul, however, he has remained himself, coarse and sexual, crude and corrupt. But he does have the power, can heal by faith, has even taken up snakes, and he has certainly felt the an-

DO, LORD, REMEMBER ME

guish of a man possessed by God. Garrett notes: "There are larger powers which he believes exist, very strongly. Every time he tries to have the power himself as separate from the mystical power that he perceives, he is put down by these and taken over, taken control of by these. So his dilemma is that whereas he has been given great gifts he can't really use them. His gifts are his undoing and, unfortunately for him, he knows it."[10] He is a familiar figure in Christian history, for, as Charles Williams pointed out, "It was laid down [in the third-century document, the *Canons of Hippolytus*] for ever that the administration of spiritual things does not depend on the character of the administrator. A man may communicate to others, and himself starve; a man may preach to others, and himself be a castaway."[11]

At the revival show, moved in flesh and spirit by the reappearance in his life of Judith, a sexually sick young woman whom he once had cured and now must try to absolve, he is overcome by God and offers even his own damnation (echoing both Matthew 25:40 and Psalm 51:8) in sacrifice for the fallen ones around him, the grotesque figures whom he loves:

> my flesh my spirit I cast like a shadow between
> You & them promising nothing asking everything

if I am damned for that then damned I am & will be

I have heard Your voice have known the beauty of ashes & oil of joy for mourning & here & now I mourn these the least & most foolish servants saying from the psalms of David also broken Thou shalt make me hear of joy & gladness that the bones which Thou has broken may rejoice (199).

Needing money, Red, Garrett notes, "intends to preach a sermon along the lines of what he believes his audience will like, a real hell-fire damnation, and the sermon gets away from him as he begins to move away from his original intention and ends up in effect teaching the gospel."[12] God intrudes on Red's plans and his sermon, ignoring Red's own needs and the perceived needs of the congregation, giving them all instead only the enigmatic sign of His presence. According to Karl Barth, "If we understand Christianity—which is, incidentally, the task of theology—in its true essence . . . we cannot close our eyes to the fact that what we have here, in antithesis to all religions, is not a human movement to God but a divine movement to humanity. . . . The so-called transcendent has become immanent before their very eyes and ears."[13]

The result of God's remembering these almost absurd characters, of His abrupt and startling

DO, LORD, REMEMBER ME

movement into this real world, the fallen world of lies, brings results as complex and enigmatic as that very movement itself: Red's revival show ends in a riot as the members of the congregation fight for the money; his associates cross and double-cross each other as guns and drugged drinks quickly switch hands; he can offer Judith a beginning only by cutting off her hair—cutting away the emblem of her sexuality, branding her a collaborator, a traitor to men and to herself; and he kills himself, drained of spirit, for reasons only God can know. The reader is left, along with the other characters of the novel, to assess what has happened and to try to make sense of it.

Red Smalley's interests are, according to Garrett, "almost totally theological, which—since he is an ex-jailbird and a ne'er do well—is kind of surprising. He's not really interested in any of the things the other people are or in what they thought he was interested in," and, of course, "what really interests him is his own personal relationship with a spirit which possesses him and overcomes him. . . . in a genuine sense in spite of himself."[14] The people in his entourage do not comprehend the nature of his spiritual problems, nor do they really understand that his is a genuine belief. Like Christ's disciples in Gethsemane, they see what is "before their very ears and eyes," but they fail to understand. Red, in a sense, sacrifices himself for them, and the terms of their continued existence offer meaning to that sacrifice even as they remain behind in their own tragicomic world of suffering and misunderstanding, absurd folly and vice.

Red's immediate entourage consists of four people whom Garrett described briefly in an interview:

It is a very poor little revival, it's no Billy Graham out there. He has collected refuse from the world. He has a rather kindly but shell-shocked veteran of WW II who is rather inept and a good man in many ways. He has a very young boy from the hills of Tennessee who is out for money—his primary interests are money and sex, about equal. They are related in some way in his mind. He has a prostitute, reformed to a degree, who is traveling with him and participates in this revival thing, and a fourth character, a girl, whom he once healed long ago, shows up again and causes a good many complications by joining them.[15]

Moses, the shell-shocked veteran, who may or may not be a Jew, is an inept protector of the Law and is the most clearly moral ("a good man in many ways") of the group. But he is scarred by the horrible memory of mistakenly slaughtering a group of schoolchildren in the war: "I have re-

DO, LORD, REMEMBER ME

mained by choice in bondage ever since. If I leave him I know those children will find me. But never here. They will not look for me here" (160).

Elijah J. Cartwright, who is known to the others as Hookworm, is the Tennessee mountain boy driven by a quest for money and sex. Humiliated and sexually injured by a relationship with Dreama the Denver Bombshell, he, "who never heard of the Magna Mater of many breasts nor Mithra either" (197), worships and fears what Dreama represents—deadly pagan sexuality, purposeless and meaningless sex. As Red puts it in a passage not included in the American edition, Cartwright seeks not just women or sex or even "the Ideal Pussy," but engages in

an endless search, a continual undressing in search of something else. Truth? No, because when he gets there, there it is. He knows what he is going to find, but he hopes he won't find it. In which case, it's the striptease, it's *the search itself* which is his idea of Truth. . . . Meaning, by this analogy, the simple platitude that we keep on going back, digging, poking, searching for the *essential*, the heart of things, knowing from the minute we start that when we get there it's going to be what we knew all the time. Wanting to find this and not wanting to at the same time. Knowing as we all slide that gleaming roller-coaster of the rainbow that there is, indeed, a pot at the end of it. It's not a pot of gold. It steams and stinks.[16]

Cartwright is the Fool or, in John Bunyan's terms, Mr. Worldly-Wise; man in his most ridiculously fallen state.

Miami, the somewhat reformed prostitute, is both Red's Mary Magdalene and his emblematic Eve, the original fallen woman. Miami, like Garrett's Salome, lives in the desert of her desires, marked by her past, but "unflinching unblinking unwinking unbelieving unbroken yet anyway still dreaming her dream of purity" (196). She shares Salome's view of hell, but, unlike Salome, she is still able to laugh and to do her dance. Early in the novel she literally dances for Howie Loomis, a local store manager, performing a striptease on his desk; and later, remembering her performance in a blue movie *Sinner's Revenge*, she reveals both her suffering and her ability to see the humor in it:

   laugh because it's absurd the unleashed human erotic imagination oh rich with folly   how many laughed not but sat silently sweating glued to these images believing it truly to be a keyhole peek at hell
   how many know what hell really is
   neither ecstasy oblivion or endless ultimate orgasm but only knowledge the simple knowledge that we are all shadows not flesh by nature unable to love ourselves or each other
   hell is the knowledge of gods

DO, LORD, REMEMBER ME

hell I have lived in will live in world without end amen but Jesus let me laugh at *Sinner's Revenge* (163).

Miami may live in a perpetual hell, but she can laugh, and she is able, for all his difficulties and betrayals to love Red: "I love him it is enough" (45).

Judith, the fourth member of Red's entourage, is the sexually sick young woman whom Red once healed years before. She comes to him again at the beginning of the novel seeking a cure for her psychic wounds that will not heal, the sexual demons that have long possessed her. If Miami is an Eve, Judith is a figuring of Lilith, the female "night monster" of Jewish folklore, the first wife of Adam who flies from him to become a demon-vampire. Lilith is generally understood to be the "screech owl" in the passage from Isaiah (34:14) which stands as the American edition's epigraph: "The wild beasts of the desert shall also meet with the wild beasts of the island, and the satyr shall cry to his fellow; the screech owl also shall rest there, and find for herself a place of rest" (iii). Judith is red-haired, fire-scarred, and tormented; to Cartwright, at one point in the novel, she "looks like some kind of a monster" (134), and Red sees her destructiveness clearly, even as he understands and shares her suffering:

> *the girl called Judith lean-legged keen-legged bearing between those scissors & matted with so soft curly hair her own cup of wormwood grail of tribulation a tight little hot little pussy with hungers beyond satisfaction with malice toward all because she was not born with two grapes & a dangling ripe banana of flesh a man so filled with destruction she will settle for nothing less than castrating every male animal in creation yet sick with guilt for this desire she offers herself her unholy grail to any & all comers in the self-abnegation & still finds no peace.*[17]

The arrival of Judith precipitates the crisis of the novel and of Red's life; he is the only man who has ever brought her even a semblance of peace, "not peace that passeth understanding but instead a brief taste of the wine of joy & gladness only a sip but enough to torment her forever" (198), and her terrible need, beyond his power to comfort or satisfy, opens him to the awful presence of God and leads him to his destructive-redemptive act of sacrifice.

In the fourth section of the novel, these four characters and Howie Loomis, the businessman for whom Miami danced, move separately into their own darkest places as the night slowly comes over the town: Cartwright into memories of

DO, LORD, REMEMBER ME

Dreama and his abasement; Moses into thoughts of the war and his guilt; Miami into thoughts of her hellish life and *Sinner's Revenge*; Loomis into a nightmare in which his dead wife does a striptease for him by peeling off her cancerous flesh; and Judith into a destructive reverie about Red in which she sees herself as the biblical Judith with the head of Holofernes or Delilah cutting the hair of Samson, but finally as a dark reflection of the lover in the Song of Songs, "bitter & more secret than the thorny rose bush" but "the water he turns into wine" (166).

As they pass through the private dark nights of their souls, Garrett describes the darkening town in terms of the primordial flood:

As if the Flood were coming on, steady and sure as those shadows. Soon they will all be drowned and from the bottom of a deep sea look up where stars bob and wink like buoys, far, far beyond the reach of townsman or traveler, remote, indifferent to their unheard cries, supercilious as the lanterns of Noah's ark, riding the crest, floating calmly towards Ararat and the inevitable, beautiful assignation of the dove and the olive branch (151).

These characters, lost in the world of lies, in the dark sea of their damnation and suffering, are in one sense actually drowning in the original flood;

as Northrop Frye notes, "In one dimension of the Deluge story the Deluge has never receded, and we still live in a submarine world of reality."[18] There "at the bottom of the sea," Moses looks up to see "the first pulsing of the evening star like a small, good diamond in the night" (167). Red's sermon and sacrifice in the immediately succeeding section of the novel function to these drowned lives, whether they recognize it immediately or not, like that evening star.

Red prays for God to love and bless his motley band of loved ones, and he offers himself as sacrifices for their salvation, echoing Jesus' language on the cross as he offered himself for all mankind:

I'm through. I'm finished. There's nothing more to say. I have said nothing but said it all in spite of myself. I have never been so tired, so empty. Is this Your plan then? To crush me with hammerblows, to drive me one blow at a time, babbling words the whole time, into the ground, one ringing blow at a time, like a poor tent peg? *Eli, Eli, lama sabachthani . . . ?* (200).

After Red's prayer, the novel moves from an ordinary world into one of heightened spirit, grotesque passion, and bawdy comedy. Cartwright's misadventures are madly funny, the downward

DO, LORD, REMEMBER ME

spiral of a born loser caught in his own worthlessness; Judith's experiences, too, including Red's cutting of her hair, are often funny, but in a darker, more pained and painful way. She and Cartwright and Moses are locked in an abandoned circus cage by Miami, where they end up dreaming, their weakness the only devil caught by Smalley's sacrifice. Miami, the fallen woman rich with life, capable of an active love and hate, escapes; Eve moves on into the world leaving Lilith in the cage, her "place of rest," drugged and dreaming, aware only that "I'm going to be sick & must be sick so I can be well" (247). The comedy ends in disaster and nightmare and violent death.

But the novel ends, not with Red's death or the caging of his friends or even with Miami's escape, but as it begins, with Howie Loomis. Miami danced for him in his office, a vulgar and ordinary striptease, as crude and sexual as animal life itself, a dance that gave him nightmares of guilt. At the novel's end, however, the dance gives Loomis another dream, one that frees him from his fears of death, that offers him a vision of human love in which all the ugliness remains but is beautiful. In essence, that dance and vision are the novel in microcosm, giving the reader Red Smalley's life and death, the world, and the dance of the imagination and spirit. Drunk and alone, Loomis dreams again of his dead wife, not a dream of purity but a dream which is at the heart of the novel and of Garrett's view of the truth that informs the world of lies:

> The light of that place and the shade too was on her. She didn't change and yet she was changed. What I mean is the light wasn't magic and it didn't wipe away any lines or scars. They remained. Yet they were beautiful. She was more beautiful than any bride. She looked at the place and smiled at it, and I looked at her and wept like a child, not for loss, but because the world was so large and so wonderful and we were both in it now and forever.
> Then the dream was gone and I was back in myself again, a drunk old man asleep on the floor. A drunk old man who had slept like a baby all night long. (253).

The dawn of another day breaks on a world as fallen as before, as drowned and as painful, but a world made somehow more bearable by love, a life made more real by the blood of continuing sacrifice, by God's awful grace.

Considering the larger work of which *Do, Lord, Remember Me* is the centerpiece as a modern version of a medieval tryptich like those of Hieronymus Bosch (and especially his *Garden of Earthly Delights*) sheds valuable light on the relationship of

DO, LORD, REMEMBER ME

the frenzied comic novella "The Satyr Shall Cry" to the other two "panels" of the work. As in a Bosch tryptich, the three parts of Garrett's trilogy portray the "vanity of the world" in increasingly more exaggerated and hellishly distorted modes. The first panel, "Noise of Strangers," portrays in traditionally realistic style and form the fall from innocence of the small Southern town of Fairview and its sheriff and protector, Jack Riddle. The tone of the story is dark and almost fatalistic, comic only incidentally, a plunge into the world of lies and the inescapable and bitter taste of the knowledge of good and evil. *Do, Lord, Remember Me* is the tragicomic center panel of the tryptich, which portrays the pain and sacrifice caused by the action of providence in the fallen world of the first panel, but portrays it with increasingly comic exaggeration—as if the very presence of belief and salvation in the world transforms its evil into merely grotesque vice and folly, cages its wickedness, and blunts its horror with a saving dream not of purity, but of wondrous recognition.

The third panel, "The Satyr Shall Cry," is on the one hand the most completely comic and on the other the most devilishly anarchistic of the three. Subtitled "A movie soundtrack in various tongues and voices,"[19] its hundred pages are divided into thirteen sections, which include spoken monologues, interior monologues, excerpts from the transcript of a trial, pages from a secret diary, a checklist of an airplane pilot, a letter from a convicted murderer to the governor, and the draft of a preface to a book of nude photographs called *The Magic Book of Woman*. Some of these sections are tonally similar to "Noise of Strangers" and others to *Do, Lord, Remember Me*, but many are in a totally new tone, pointedly satirical while exhibiting Chaucerian bawdiness with the slapstick speed of a series of burlesque turns. The plot is an elaborate crisscross of complex cause and effect, with each character possessing his or her own theory about who or what is to blame for the disasters that smite the town of Paradise Springs, Florida. The various stories they tell weave a pattern of corroboration and contradiction that lead the baffled reader to agree with Sheriff Dave Prince that the possibility of understanding patterns and discovering causal connections in human affairs is about the same as that in subatomic physics:

I don't really believe in cause and effect. That's just an idea, a convenience which can be used in trying to describe and to understand some aspects of human relations. But to take that convenient idea and try to apply it, literally and seriously, to the unhuman

DO, LORD, REMEMBER ME

universe is just plain silly. No, it's more than that. It's crazy.

Try and deal with something like subatomic physics in terms of cause and effect and you will see what I mean.

. . . There are, to my knowledge, a whole lot of unconnected events, crazy-ass stuff, that happened here in the county all at the same time. And . . . they don't seem to relate to each other in any conventional way. But the more I think about it—and, as you can see, a lot of the time I have time to think about things—the more it all seems to be part of some weirdo pattern.

Sometimes I think about that and then I find myself thinking that maybe the pattern is the only real thing and that all the details are, well, interchangeable, maybe even irrelevant. You know? (179-80).

The "weirdo pattern" that Sheriff Prince intuitively feels is "the only real thing" is the pattern of the story that repeats itself in all three panels of the tryptich: the destructive intrusion of an outside reality into the life of a small town that tears away the veils of illusion behind which the naked truth has been concealed and forces the people involved to face the truth and themselves in the fallen world of lies. Garrett sees this pattern as the central fact of human experience ("the only real thing"), essential to any possibility of individual

UNDERSTANDING GEORGE GARRETT

moral life or spiritual salvation. The sheriff does not, of course, recognize the pattern for what it is, just as he cannot know (despite the metafictional quality of "The Satyr Shall Cry") that he has also accurately described the structure and method of the fictional tryptich in which he is a character.

The town may be called Fairview or High Pines or Paradise Springs, but the pattern of events that occur there repeats itself in each panel of the tryptich, and the primary characters do, too (especially in the latter two panels). The names and specific characteristics change, but the place of the characters in the pattern identifies them almost archetypally. Sheriff Jack Riddle ("Noise of Strangers") becomes Sheriff Jack Starr in *Do, Lord Remember Me* and Sheriff Dave Prince in "The Satyr Shall Cry." Mr. Percy, a prissy store clerk and minor character in *Do, Lord, Remember Me,* becomes the centrally important photographer Martin Pressy in "The Satyr Shall Cry." The itinerant Ike Toombs is transformed into the evangelist Red Smalley, who in turn reappears as Dan Lee Smithers,

also known as Little David, an itinerant revivalist preacher, estimated to be in his late thirties or early forties, but so small and delicate of bone and stature, so pure and high in speaking and singing voice, so

DO, LORD, REMEMBER ME

unlined and unblemished of skin and complexion, that (with the aid of proper cosmetics and costume and a gold, curly wig) he could pass for a child, a prodigy chosen by the Lord to be blessed with the gift of tongues and a healing touch (176).

The characters and events in *Do, Lord, Remember Me* and "The Satyr Shall Cry" recur particularly clearly: Cartwright becomes Billy Papp, "alias 'Billygoat' and 'Goathead' " (176); Moses is transformed into Raphael Cone, a black man this time; Judith appears as Alpha Weatherby, a young woman who, after posing nude for Martin Pressy, "started doing weird things like not wearing any underwear" (188) and enters a state of desperate religious-sexual confusion and demonic vision; and Miami becomes Geneva Laseur (born Bertha Frond), who "stands well over six feet barefooted and weighs easily as much as many professional football players" (177). Another character, Darlene Blaze, also shares much of Miami's nature. The new mix of characters, much more overtly grotesque and comic, also results in disaster; the evangelist again cuts the psychologically wounded girl's hair, but this time both she and he are shot and killed in a chaotic shoot-out with Geneva Laseur. The mix is stirred this time by the townspeople, especially Alpha Weatherby's devilish little brother, Penrose; Martin Pressy, the photographer; and Professor Moses Katz, a hustling phony academic at the local college (who is forerunner of Jack Towne, the academic con man of *Poison Pen*).

The story repeats itself in a tangle of confused and confusing events, a distorted mirror image of the form it took in *Do, Lord, Remember Me*, a comic hell of vice and folly without hope of redemption. Martin Pressy's career as a photographer is an accurate microcosm of the madness of the novella: his descent from surreptitiously photographing nudes for his *The Magic Book of Woman* to photographing the dead bodies of Little David and Alpha to his ultimate art, photographing corpses killed in highway crashes. The life in the novella takes a similar dizzying descent into madness and death and absurdity. Only Geneva Laseur's letter to the governor after she has been convicted of murder, asking his pardon for all the trouble she has, however accidentally, caused, has anything of charity in it; Eve, the mother of us all, can still speak something like the truth in this hellish world, can at least say that "one day I will shed my weary flesh and bones like old clothes and then my heart will be light again. I will be so light I can float on the air" (272). She asks the governor to send her body to her sister in Texas for burial,

DO, LORD, REMEMBER ME

giving her "a chance to make up for what she hasn't done and to feel better about herself." And she adds, "Don't we all need a chance for something like that?" (272).

The tryptich formed by these two novellas and the novel is, again like the Bosch tryptich, a Christian view of life in a fallen world, one in which vice and folly reign and in which there can be no earthly paradise. The divine presence of redemption and salvation moves through the world, but it is rendered almost unrecognizable by the distorting mirrors of the world of lies. Only in acts of love and sacrifice may the truth beyond the naked truth of the world be known. Garrett, like so many Christian artists before him, expresses his understanding of this complex world in a tragicomic mode, seeing that world as tragic in its continuing submission to sin and death, and comic in its absurd failure to recognize that it has already been redeemed from sin and death by divine love.

The editors who cut the larger novel before publishing it and the critics who failed to identify the novel's true coherence and identity did Garrett's readers a great disservice. Until the time that the text of the entire work may be published, however, the tryptich may be reconstructed with a little effort by readers who are willing to do some looking around in libraries and secondhand bookstores. The result of their efforts will be the discovery of a major American novel.

Notes

1. John Graham and W. R. Robinson, "George Garrett Discusses Writing and His Work," *Mill Mountain Review* 1 (1971): 93-94.

2. George Garrett, *An Evening Performance* (Garden City: Doubleday, 1985) 473. Further references to short fiction will be to this edition unless otherwise noted and will be noted parenthetically.

3. Graham and Robinson 92.

4. Graham and Robinson 93.

5. Garrett, *Cold Ground Was My Bed Last Night* (Columbia: University of Missouri Press, 1964) 147.

6. Graham and Robinson 94.

7. Garrett, *Do, Lord, Remember Me* (London: Chapman and Hall, 1965) 5.

8. Garrett, *Do, Lord, Remember Me* (Garden City: Doubleday, 1965) vii. Further references are to this edition unless otherwise noted and will be noted parenthetically.

9. *The Collected Poems of George Garrett* (Fayetteville: University of Arkansas Press, 1984) 15-16. Further references to poems will be to this edition and will be noted parenthetically.

10. Graham and Robinson 95.

11. Charles Williams, *The Descent of the Dove: A Short History of the Holy Spirit in the Church* (New York: Oxford University Press, 1939) 43.

12. Graham and Robinson 94.

13. Rolf Jaochim Erler and Reiner Marquard, *A Karl Barth Reader* (Grand Rapids: Eerdmans, 1986) 29.

14. Graham and Robinson 94, 93.

15. Graham and Robinson 94.

DO, LORD, REMEMBER ME

16. Garrett, *Do, Lord, Remember Me* (British ed.) 189-90.

17. Garrett, *Do, Lord, Remember Me* (British ed.) 220-21.

18. Northrop Frye, *The Great Code: The Bible and Literature* (New York: Harcourt Brace, 1982) 192.

19. Garrett, *The Magic Striptease* (Garden City: Doubleday, 1973) 173. Further references will be noted parenthetically.

CHAPTER FIVE

The Elizabethan Novels: *Death of the Fox* and *The Succession*

George Garrett's first three novels develop his exploration of the fallen world of lies in a coherent and distinctive manner, revealing his special concerns and primary themes clearly, but they are also novels that belong to and grow from a familiar tradition. The literary influences that helped shape them are readily identifiable: Faulkner and Warren in *The Finished Man*, Hemingway and Salinger in *Which Ones Are the Enemy?* and, to a lesser degree, Faulkner again in *Do, Lord, Remember Me.* They are not derivative novels in the sense that they imitate or attempt to repeat exactly the successes of their literary forebears, but they do clearly have antecedents in the work of that gener-

THE ELIZABETHAN NOVELS

ation of novelists who immediately preceded Garrett. Garrett's next two novels, his major Elizabethan historical novels, *Death of the Fox* and *The Succession*, break away completely from what has gone before them and constitute something utterly new in the history of the novel. As Monroe K. Spears noted, they "are such remarkable historical novels that they may be considered either fulfillments of the genre or repudiations of it."[1]

The two books are recognizably "historical" novels. The first deals with the events leading up to and surrounding the execution of Sir Walter Ralegh in 1618; the second, with events ranging from the birth of King James in 1566 to the succession of Charles in 1625, pivoting on the crucial succession of James to the throne of Queen Elizabeth in 1603. But both novels refuse to give readers what they might expect from historical fiction, which for the most part has changed very little from Sir Walter Scott's *Waverly* (1814) to Norman Mailer's *Ancient Evenings* (1983), and gives them instead a great deal more—a fiction of artistic subtlety and intelligence rather than of derring-do, of living fact rather than antiquarian gesture, of imaginative meditation on history rather than the recounting of invented events against a backdrop of history. Garrett builds up a historical context of great richness and factual accuracy—an Elizabethan and Jacobean

THE ELIZABETHAN NOVELS

world which is fully researched and vividly rendered—but he abandons conventional plot along with almost all of the other conventions of the genre in a successful effort to create new narrative forms, "open texts" which engage readers in the very act of historical imagination and allow them direct access to what Garrett calls "the larger imagination, the possibility of imagining lives and spirits of other human beings, living or dead, without assaulting their essential and, anyway, ineffable mystery, to dream again in recapitulation the dream of Adam, knowing, as he did not until he awoke, that it is true."[2]

In a prefatory note to an early draft of *Death of the Fox* (called at that time "Stars Must Fall"), Garrett indicated both his awareness of the difficulties he felt that his new formal innovations would have with conservative critics and readers, and his conviction that he was truly exploring fertile new ground for the novel as a vital literary form:

You may call this narrative what you please. I choose to call it a novel, acknowledging that there are those who would and will disagree with me. I call it that because it is long enough, because it is chiefly a work of fiction, and because—and here I have some pretty good company, if a minority—I happen to think that the "rules" by which we once used to identify one narrative form or another, are out of date, inapplicable

THE ELIZABETHAN NOVELS

to much that has been written and has been read. And because I do not for one minute think that the novel is "dead." In some ways, thanks to the great pioneers of the form in our time, we are only just beginning to map and survey the territory. In some cases we ourselves are explorers, for the masters have left much that is labeled *terra incognita*.[3]

Garrett's explorations into the unknown land of the "larger imagination" led him from the known ground of his personal experience in the American South and the U.S. Army into the distant world of the Renaissance and Elizabethan England, a world he had entered imaginatively through the poetry of Sir Walter Ralegh and had come to know intellectually during his graduate studies at Princeton. His original plan to write a formal biography of Ralegh for his doctoral dissertation transmuted itself into these two novels, both of which are re-creations of that distant world but are even more importantly celebrations and demonstrations of "the human imagination, the possibility, limits and variety of imaginative experience."[4]

In order to make that exploration of the human imagination a genuine venture into *terra incognita*, Garrett realized that "to be interesting to work on over a length of time, and, as it happens, to be true to my feelings for the man [Ralegh] and the

THE ELIZABETHAN NOVELS

times, my work would have to be different from any I had known or enjoyed,"[5] and to that end he made a number of aesthetic decisions and developed a set of rules to guide his imaginative effort. Convinced that he could come to know the man and the times by a direct act of the imagination without an overlay of contemporary concerns and interests, he rejected "the alternative of 'relevance' or satire." He would, despite his admiration for Edith Sitwell's *Fanfare for Elizabeth* and Marguerite Yourcenar's *Hadrian's Memoirs*, not opt for "the 'poetic' manner." He would not attempt to fill in the blank spaces or mysteries of Ralegh's life with imagined detail, "attributing one motive or another for the seemingly inexplicable action," but would rather "accept them as inherent mysteries." He would "though allowing myself the freedom of all imaginative work . . . keep to the decorum of fact except in very rare cases where it seemed to me that the evidence was sufficient to be more definite than speculative." Admitting the value of scholarly studies of the ideas of the period, he nevertheless determined that "ideas, the history of ideas, would be building blocks, not excluded, but not dominating the work." And finally he determined to develop a new style, one "which will serve to conjure up the ghosts and ruins for the writer and, rhetorically, permit the reader to par-

THE ELIZABETHAN NOVELS

ticipate in this incantation," in the direction of the intensely personal and "therefore eccentric" style of James Joyce in *Finnegans Wake* or Djuna Barnes in *Ryder*, but "with the private stipulation that the language must be readable, at least within the context of the work, accessible to an imaginary reader."[6]

In his prefaces to the two novels Garrett reduced the statement of his complex aesthetic decisions and rules still further. In the note to *Death of the Fox*, emphasizing the organic relationship between his imaginative work and the fertile soil of history, he says, "I wanted to make a work of fiction, of the imagination, planted and rooted in fact. I wanted facts to feed and give strength to the truths of fiction."[7] *Death of the Fox* makes that organic relationship clear both because it is centered in the life and spirit of one man, Sir Walter Ralegh, and because that man was, in addition to all of his other characteristics and identities, a historian and an artist—a poet and literary imaginer as well as a scholar and man of action. In the note to *The Succession*, a novel without a hero or even a central character, Garrett explains that his effort to contemplate the complex relationship of Queen Elizabeth and King James through their correspondence led him to examine and imagine many other characters who "must be allowed to tell their own

THE ELIZABETHAN NOVELS

tales also."[8] The result is a novel less clearly organic and more complex than its predecessor, one in which the truth is less focused, one no longer concerned with the meaning of one man's life in his times but rather with meaning itself, with time itself, with life itself. For this larger task Garrett developed an even more radical form, but one still grounded in his rules, one in which "I have done my best to be faithful to the facts even while striving to preserve the freedom of fiction, which means that there may be distortions and there will be mistakes, but I hope there are no lies" (viii).

Spears has accurately described the distinctive characteristics of these two novels which are the product of Garrett's exploration of the "possibility, limits and variety of imaginative experience":

Garrett . . . doesn't take any easy outs: his central characters are historical and are involved in centrally important historical events, which are followed meticulously in the novels. No liberties are taken with the facts: Garrett invents narrative detail but changes nothing and adds only what is plainly justified by analogy. Since the main characters are historical and the reader knows in advance what happened to them, there can be no narrative suspense. . . . The characters are always presented in depth from the inside. Though there is a great variety of perspectives, points of view, and kinds of interest in the different sections, the unifying attitude and tone are contemplative and

THE ELIZABETHAN NOVELS

meditative. Garrett's attitude toward the past is neither romantic nor debunking: he has a marvelous sense of ceremony, ritual, and pageantry, and of the immense significance of these things—and, of course, of religion—to the characters (in implicit contrast to moderns). . . . There is no explicit comparison to our own "real" world (though much implicit); Garrett never intrudes in his own person, but always speaks through the imagined mind of a "historical" personage or "ghost."[9]

Spears is correct that Garrett never "intrudes" in his own person in the novels, but he is very much present in the text of *Death of the Fox* as a diegetic narrative voice (that of the teller of the tale), one that guides the reader deeply into the world of the novel and into the mind of Sir Walter Ralegh, and that ultimately achieves imaginative fusion with Ralegh's own voice in the climactic scene of the novel. In *The Succession*, lacking as it does a central character, the narrative stance is more fully mimetic in the way that Spears indicates. In both novels, through his careful research into Elizabethan life and the particular lives of his historical characters, the Christian belief which he shares with those characters, and the power of his craft and art, Garrett does succeed in bringing a lost past to imaginative life; and he thereby allows his readers an opportunity not only to share that res-

THE ELIZABETHAN NOVELS

urrected world but to experience the force and power of the fully committed imagination.

Death of the Fox

According to Gertrude Stein, the only way that historical novels and plays or, for that matter, the writing of history itself can be literature is for the writer to imagine his or her characters so completely that "the only existing the character has is the character the writer has given to them." She goes on to speak of the near impossibility of the task because of "all the audience that has known every one about whom he is writing. . . . It is worse than the wailing of the dead soldiers in L'Aiglon there are so many auditors . . . and how can he lose all of them and if he does not how can history be writing that is literature."[10] The writer's task, in other words, is to write about a subject everyone knows and to imagine that subject so fully that readers lose all sense of what they already know and discover the subject completely anew.

Death of the Fox is a novel in which George Garrett fulfills Stein's description of the writer's task, a novel in which the historical Sir Walter Ra-

DEATH OF THE FOX

legh and the fading Elizabethan world around him in his last days (28-29 October 1618) take on fictive life, become a living man and a living world, colorful, detailed, and exact. The Ralegh of history and legend is subsumed into the Ralegh on the page, the fully imagined and rendered interior Ralegh who takes life in the text and the reader's awakened imagination. But, perhaps more important, it is a novel of the present living moment, of that moment's flow into history as it transforms the future into itself. The past lives naturally as the texture from which the present shapes itself, and Garrett's novel is an expression not only of a dreamed and re-created past, but also of that act of creation itself, the imaginative moment that gives time conscious being.

"All memory," Ralegh thinks to himself as he sits in the Tower, musing on last things on his next to last day on this earth, "is vain and foolish and all history compounded of many memories, therefore all the more vain and foolish. Yet a man could do worse than remember such times" (555). Ralegh remembers those times, and Garrett builds a texture of the memories of others around him as well. The reader shares the thoughts, dreams, and memories of such historical figures as King James, Henry Yelverton, Sir Allan Apsley, Sir Francis Ba-

THE ELIZABETHAN NOVELS

con, and many others, including Ralegh's executioner, Gregory Brandon. As Ralegh nods by the fire after hearing his death sentence, Garrett also calls upon the testimony of three "ghosts"—a soldier, a courtier, and a sailor—to present Ralegh's complex and multiform world and his place in it more fully:

Time, while the old man dozes, to summon up ghosts, imagined and imaginary. Nameless except for their roles and stations.
    Perhaps he will not be offended if they are to be considered *characters* in the fashion of the types of Englishmen drawn by Sir Thomas Overbury. Who showed more wit in his book of *Characters* than he did in his appetite for sweet tarts.
    Perhaps Ralegh may ignore an interlude with imaginary ghosts, since they are nameless and of no more dimension than figures in tapestry or stained cloth (254).

These imagined "ghosts" and imagined historical figures populate a world which is in part ghostly itself, for the lost Elizabethan world still casts its brightness over the faded luster of the Jacobean landscape and renders its reality suspect even in the minds of those who are shaping it. Ralegh is, in one sense, the last Elizabethan, and his death is intended to function as an exorcism to those of the

DEATH OF THE FOX

new era, who feel that they must lay all the Elizabethan ghosts in order to assert their own substantiality and worth.

The "ghosts" and Ralegh, however, remember that departed Elizabethan world and bring it back to life for the reader fully dimensioned. It was a "time of color and wonder in England from which even the poorest and most humble were not quite forbidden or spared," "a false garden, forever new and changing" (554). It was a time of poetry to be followed by a time of prose; it was a time seemingly out of time, freed of past and future in its own unbelievably bright presence:

Time was as the tides of the river for us. We rode it, floated upon it like the Queen's barge. Her barge was a glorious thing with gleaming brightwork, awnings of cloth of gold, silken pillows and lacquered oars, and it was pulled steady and skilled by a crew in royal livery. Her barge moved down the river, fireworks fountaining explosions overhead, kettledrums beating, trumpets sounding proud and clear across the river. Her barge in moonlight, riding the Thames, that is a proper figure for our time (554–55).

This "false garden" was, according to Garrett, the product of Elizabeth's deep conservatism, her desire not to repeat the mistakes of Henry VIII in

THE ELIZABETHAN NOVELS

attempting to master the future nor those of Mary in attempting to restore the past:

> Freed from concern about the future by circumstance and by choice, schooling herself in the past and aiming to recover rather than to restore, she found herself oddly free to live (dangerously) in a continual present. And so, ironically, possessed a longer future and a longer past than any other monarch before her. Yet while England burned with change, turn and counterturn for half a century, it was, we can see now, a time of relative sameness and stability. And with her death that inner quiet, persistent at the heart of outer clamor, died too. To be followed, as surely, by England's deluge. Which, if true, means finally that whether she wished it so or not, her refusal to commit herself to the future made that future inevitable.[11]

Elizabeth created the "false garden" of peace and stability, one that could not, by the very nature of things, last; and yet by that illusion she gave the prosaic and unstable future a measure by which to understand and judge itself and created a truth through and beyond the illusion. The Elizabethans lived in that paradoxical context of truth and illusion completely; Garrett demonstrates how their extravagant clothes and manners, their homes and dinners and pompous displays, were all part and parcel of the larger creation of the world of the

DEATH OF THE FOX

Queen. They created an illusion of a great England and thereby made England great. Able to tell truth from fancy, they were able to manipulate fancy toward the creation of truth. They were, in short, poets.

In the novel Ralegh remembers the living poetry of that world and identifies love—Elizabeth's love for her people and theirs for her—as the source of its poetry and its lasting qualities even in an age of prose:

We deprived her of her youth, forbade her from the life and natural joy of a woman, and in the end denied her even the privilege to be old.

That she loved us and this kingdom I find remarkable. Yet she did love us and even at the last when so few loved her.

And it is that love . . . all these years afterwards, which has the power to transform our memory of her, of the age, and therefore of ourselves. So that we view those times gone with and through the transforming power of love. And none of us who were witnesses in the flesh, will ever again have the power to give true testimony.

We are all false witnesses. Yet the sum of our witnessing may be true (529).

Ralegh at the end, Ralegh remembering the poetry and the truth of his time and times, that is

THE ELIZABETHAN NOVELS

the subject of the novel—an old and beaten man, the last Elizabethan, awaiting and experiencing his final hearing, his condemnation and his execution, realizing in the face of the end that his life was wasted and that the world he lived it in and for was "false, illusory, chimerical, bewitched, enchanted" (555). He thinks, "I could easily curse myself and my wasted days" (555), but he does not. He chooses to die as he lived, to act upon his values even as they ring false at the end, to recreate those values by his actions in the minds of those who will live after him, to make those false values true by the life which his death will give them.

That has long been the puzzle of Sir Walter Ralegh: why he chose to die the way he did at the hands of a king he loathed and with such Elizabethan style in a time without style or understanding of style. Garrett's Ralegh dies, not with the rational self-assurance of Socrates, but with the imaginative assurance of a poet. "True or false," he thinks, his time "was a glorious springtime" (555), and he will not allow himself to betray the aesthetic rightness of that springtime. With a poet's faith in his craft and art he chooses the truth that is beautiful, and with an artist's moral strength he alters the composition of the time beyond him to make that beauty true. With a Christian's faith he

DEATH OF THE FOX

knows that the truth *is* beautiful and the composition true:

There is a pattern and design in any man's actions, in the chronicle of his words, thoughts and deeds, which is an image, apelike, of the larger sum and total of the acts, the thoughts and deeds of all men. Which we call history. What was, is, will be. And its secret design is Providence. Which we can come to know only by and through contraries and paradoxes.
Intricate beyond comprehending, it speaks of a beautiful simplicity (173).

It is this faith, grounded both aesthetically and spiritually, that enables Ralegh to complete his life as he does, that enables him to bear what his old age has brought him, and to discover (and create) a victory in his defeat. Thinking of the old Queen's looking glasses—the mirrors which she ordered covered in all public rooms where she might pass and the mirrors with which she surrounded herself in her bath—he comes to an understanding of her private honesty with herself and a larger understanding of the human condition. Like Howie Loomis at the end of *Do, Lord, Remember Me*, he attains a vision of the beauty that is present in suffering and disfigurement, in life in the fallen world of lies, of the purity that exists in the desert:

THE ELIZABETHAN NOVELS

Still in all, I think no man is so loathsome that, even in self-disgust, he cannot cleave to the belief that in some way, magical, as in some myth or child's tale of transformation, toad into prince, sow's ear into silk purse and the like, that in some way he is far more beautiful than he seems or knows. I venture there is a hidden truth veiled behind this illusion. We are said to be in the image of God—which we take to be the soul eternal and not the corrupted and corruptible flesh—and to be in the image of God, is, therefore, to be beautiful. And therefore the naked truth of us, veiled though it is, is beautiful, and would be most beautiful if we could behold it. This illusion, then, though it be denied by every wrinkle and deformity of flesh, may be the one true apprehension of our true condition. It is a sad wish that is more than a wish, because what it asks for has already been granted (526–27).

Secure in that vision, Ralegh, by his words and actions, participates in the creation of the world that will follow his own, and, in *Death of the Fox*, he creates the world around him as well. He makes it real by imagining it with an imagination honed by experience and fully grounded in fact; that imaginative creation of the present gives him the necessary depth of vision to set about creating the future. He is taken by way of the Thames to his final trial, and on the way he creates a London, the London he sees and hears and smells and the Lon-

DEATH OF THE FOX

don he remembers and knows to be real beyond the reach of his senses. Memory and imagining mingle with the sensations of physical fact to create the mystery of the living moment:

He sighs for the shimmering, evanescent, butterfly's wing of the present moment. Which reason again reminds him is his most precious possession. That moment, in purity, always threatened by memory and wishes. Or is that true? Why not call the present the sum of all?
 The trick of time lies in its deceptions. Pea in the pod, shell game, past, present, future, shift place in one instant and who can say which is which and be sure? (203–04)

The moment may be mystery, but people give it reality by daring to *see* it and to *imagine* it. They give it conscious reality; they make it fact, and fact is, as Einstein suggested, as subjective as fancy and as true.

Ralegh sees the world and dreams it; King James allows the world to dream him, and he crushes his glasses in his hand that he may not have to see the world that gives him his reality:

Where he has been, what he has dreamed, he cannot remember. Some part of it seems to have been at the Tower, that fearful place whose first foundations were tempered by the clotted blood of slaughtered beasts.

THE ELIZABETHAN NOVELS

In the dream Henry was alive and well. Christian of Denmark was there too. The keeper was baiting one of the lions with bear hounds. But it was a sad lion that would not fight the dogs. The dogs were all snarls and teeth like knives. The sad lion looked at him. A lion with his own face . . .
 Then he was somewhere else. He cannot remember where. Only that, cold sweat on him, it was dreadful as hell itself (103).

James forces himself awake, but his hand dreams on, acting on what he has allowed himself to become, and crushes his glasses. The King, eased and comforted by his faithful Steenie, "feels lightheaded, drunk with emptiness" (104). He disappears into emptiness; he becomes only what we will make of him. But Ralegh imagines himself fully into a substantial world of breath and fact; dream of him what we may, his own imagination imposes itself upon our dreams, the reality of his vision becomes our fact.

Some of the most vividly rendered scenes in the novel occur not at the level of narrative fact or in the narrative present, but are imagined by Ralegh; Ralegh, the man without a future, imagines the future of others, how they will behave in the days after his death. He pictures Sir Thomas Wilson's futile efforts to take possession of his valuable books and instruments, foiled by Apsley. He

DEATH OF THE FOX

pictures his kinsman and betrayer, Stukely, eaten up by fear and guilt and finding no comfort in the King's bag of gold, staring at his own face reflected in a rain-washed window, weeping and thinking, "A man is drowning out there" (457). And he pictures Sir Francis Bacon hosting a dinner, surrounded with his fourteen-year-old bride by elaborate jeweled objects, his philosophical materialism reflected in his gadgets: a complicated clock with a combative Crusader and Saracen, and a cunningly contrived silver ship which moves by clockwork with each cannon firing a different-colored smoke.

Bacon, who lives in fear of providence and who has only "a faith of this world, faith in the King he serves and in those who serve him" with "no faith left for himself" (503), stands as Ralegh's mirror image, his Jacobean double, lost in materialism and fear, unable to face the future. Even as Ralegh imagines Bacon, he finds in himself his own vision of the future and of the Kingdom of Heaven, knowing "that we never left home but only dreamed a dream of faring forth and returning; that we shall not be welcomed as returning, but rather greeted as if waking from a sleep and a dream; and that we shall be greeted in a language we understand, having always known it" (501). Ralegh imagines Bacon and finds himself, just as

THE ELIZABETHAN NOVELS

he imagines the prosaic world around him and finds proof of the poetic world he has lost and must re-create in his death. Ralegh's imagination allows him to know himself and his future and to fear neither. Unlike King James or Bacon, he has nothing unknown to fear, nothing that he is unable to imagine and come to terms with in his faith; and unlike them, he is able to go peacefully to sleep unhaunted by nightmares. The man without a future has the richest future of them all.

Jorge Luis Borges remarks that "a man sets himself the task of portraying the world," but that "shortly before his death, he discovers that the patient labyrinth of lines traces the image of his face."[12] But he also says, in his essay on the mysterious collaboration across the centuries of Omar Khayyám and Edward FitzGerald, that "all collaboration is mysterious," and that "death and vicissitudes and time caused one to know of the other and made them into a single poet."[13] The collaboration between Ralegh and George Garrett is as mysterious. Ralegh dreams his world and makes it real as he is himself being dreamed by Garrett, but in a dream shaped by Ralegh's words and deeds. Ralegh's London and its inhabitants bear the faces Ralegh gives them, but they also trace the face of Ralegh. And both that London and that Ralegh

DEATH OF THE FOX

trace the face of Garrett. And, of course, Garrett does know the terms of this mysterious collaboration which is at the very heart of his exploration of the "larger imagination."

The early draft of the novel, "Stars Must Fall," has a modern narrator, a man sitting in a boathouse in Maine (where Garrett has a house and a boathouse) who is called only "the Professor." This character, the ostensible author of the book, stands "in a sense . . . between you and the tale. His shadow falls between you and the people, their actions, the events which, joined together, become a story." He is a man "alone with paper and pen and books, alone with his mind, with five senses and the steady rhythm of his pulse, . . . *hoping to summon up a company of ghosts and strangers.*"[14] Later in the novel the Professor admits that, in his imaginative struggle to imagine Ralegh and his time, "I wrestle ghosts and angels. They all have my own face."[15] His dilemma depends upon his attempt to imagine another time without imposing on it his modern face and his modern preoccupations, a task made especially difficult by his sense that the modern world has become so detached from reality that "we cannot now even imagine *ourselves.* Except in bits and pieces. . . . Do we dare even to imagine a wholeness or a dream of wholeness

THE ELIZABETHAN NOVELS

when our safety seems to lie in its absence? Absence of thought, absence of feeling."[16]

Garrett resolved the Professor's dilemma by removing him from the novel, removing his shadow from between the reader and the events, and by bringing the act of the imagination, the collaboration between Ralegh and Garrett, to the very center and heart of the novel:

I came to cling to the notion that the proper subject and theme of historical fiction is what it is—the human imagination in action, itself dramatized as it struggles with surfaces, builds structures with facts, deals out and plays a hand of ideas, and most of all, by conceiving of the imagination of others, wrestles with the angel (Wallace Stevens' "necessary angel") of the imagination.[17]

The Professor disappears from the novel, but the angel of Garrett's imagination (who has his face) takes an even more important role. Garrett celebrates his own imagination even as he creates Ralegh on the page, for what better celebration is there than the imaginative act itself? His celebration of the larger imagination is the complex result of the fusion of Garrett's and Ralegh's sensibilities in the novel, in the imaginative fact of *Death of the Fox*. Like FitzGerald and Khayyám, Garrett and Ralegh become a single poet, Ralegh shaping the

DEATH OF THE FOX

material that feeds Garrett's imagination, which in turns reshapes that material into the novel.

W. R. Robinson pointed out the close relationship between Ralegh and the central characters of Garrett's first three novels: Mike Royle, the courtier; John Riche, the soldier; Big Red Smalley, the believer and spiritual explorer. Robinson noted that "actually, since the first three novels were written during the period during which Garrett was searching for the form for *Death of the Fox* they constitute exploratory efforts toward what is consummated, at least for the time being, there. And, in fact, Garrett does deliver the man that had been struggling to be born through his earlier novels. . . . He [Ralegh] is the whole man of which they were fragments."[18] Ralegh is the fullest expression of Garrett's quest for the fully imagined individual, giving him the opportunity to bring the central concerns of his poetry and fiction together in a single culminating work, and freeing him to do work of a very different kind in the years to follow.

Ralegh writes one last long letter of advice to his son Carew in part 5 of *Death of the Fox*, the substance of the historical Ralegh shaped into imaginative fact. But it is more than the re-creation of an unsent and possibly even unwritten letter by Ralegh, for it is an open fusion on the page of Ra-

THE ELIZABETHAN NOVELS

legh and Garrett, an explicit revelation of that fusion which is the novel as a whole. The letter winds through some forty-eight pages, a distillation of the historical Ralegh's writings and a summation of his imagined meditations in the novel. But its conclusion is a close paraphrase of Garrett's poem "For My Sons"—the poem filtered through Ralegh's imagined sensibility and emerging in Ralegh's prose, the shared advice of two fathers separated by centuries to their sons:

> For the world, I leave you a small inheritance and less wisdom.
> Do not think much on my own guilt or innocence or the justice of the world. Live and think only that justice is in the world. Believe that.
> Small wisdom and that only in old words. Words no more than sweet comfits to lighten the taste of dust on the tongue.
> Nothing stings like the serpent. No pain greater. Bear it.
> If a bush should burn and the flames cry out, bow down.
> If ever a stranger wrestle you, do not let go until you learn his name.
> If after long voyages, tossing and fever, you find a new continent, plant your flags proudly. Stand tall. Send forth a dove.
> Rarely the fruit you reach for shall return your love (563).

DEATH OF THE FOX

Ralegh destroys the letter, but Garrett writes it for him again 350 years later. Ralegh and Garrett become in this passage more than mirrors set up each to each; they become a single poet, or at least sharers of a most mysterious and meaningful collaboration. And that collaboration and that unity are the fullest celebration of the larger imagination.

What allows Garrett the opportunity for this full collaboration with Ralegh across the centuries is their shared belief. Both Ralegh and Garrett are Christian artists: Ralegh in an overtly Christian age when the terms of Christian belief were inherent in the thought of the time; Garrett in (to use W. H. Auden's term) an age of anxiety, a secular age without shared belief.

Ralegh designs the end of his life, the manner of his leaving it, with the care of a poet finishing a poem. He finishes it in Christian terms, just as he had finished the night before an old poem, one years old which had been playing along the edges of his mind all day long, one which lacked a proper ending:

> Even such is time which takes in trust
> Our youth, our joys, our all we have
> And pays us but with age and dust;

THE ELIZABETHAN NOVELS

> Who in the dark and silent grave
> When we have wandered all our ways
> Shuts up the story of our days.
> But from this earth, this grave, this dust,
> My God shall raise me up I trust (611–12).

The poem ends with faith and hope, and Ralegh ends his life, as any Christian would hope to, in imitation of Christ. He chooses the cup that must come, and he forgives himself the sins of his past in the surety of the mercy to come. He does not curse himself and die; he dies at ease with himself and with God.

Garrett enriches the imitation of Christ of Ralegh's death with a pattern of Christian symbols and echoes. Ralegh faces his unfair last trial, he shares his last supper, he finds his Judas in his kinsman Stukely, and he speaks his own version of Christ's last words to his executioner: "What doest thou fear? Strike, man, strike!" (739). These are Ralegh's historical last words set in an imaginative and consciously Christian context by Ralegh's modern collaborator. Garrett, then, celebrates the imagination that shapes the whole of the living world, and his novel becomes a prayer of praise to that divine imagination.

Garrett's journey into the past frees him to the present; in the hard-earned recovery of spirit in

DEATH OF THE FOX

lost and irrecoverable fact, he finds the wisdom (speaking through Ralegh) to believe in the future of humankind:

The pagan poets and philosophers, perceiving that the world can only grow older in time, divided all time into four ages, each of a baser metal than the last. And there is much truth in the figure. Yet it can never be truly apt while the world still lives. For if the history of man has its ages like the seasons, then, like the seasons, they must turn and return, be revived as well (554).

Death of the Fox, an exploration and celebration of the larger imagination, renews as well the genre of historical fiction, gives it a life in American literature that it has seldom had. It is also a book with largeness of spirit in a time of spiritual exhaustion. Garrett's imaginative examination of the individual uncovered for him the possibilities of coherence and wholeness even as he was writing in an incoherent and fragmented time; it freed him to explore beyond the self in *The Succession* and *Poison Pen* into the web of consciousness that shapes all public life, secure in the ground he discovered in this novel, the ground of the believing and loving self, knowing with Ralegh that "so long as the heart is right, it is no matter which way the head lies" (738).

THE ELIZABETHAN NOVELS

The Succession

In her first major breakthrough into radical form, *Tender Buttons*, Gertrude Stein uttered the imperative: "Act so that there is no use in a centre."[19] In his second Elizabethan historical novel, *The Succession*, Garrett breaks through himself, developing a form much more radical than that of *Death of the Fox*, denying himself the unifying element of a dominant central character, moving beyond events to the creation of meaning in events, opening the novel to the study of meaning itself: acting, in other words, as Stein demanded, so that there is no use in a center.

The Succession is, as its subtitle claims, "A Novel of Elizabeth and James," a re-creation of the complex events surrounding the succession of James I to the throne of Queen Elizabeth. It is a historical novel; it does cover much of the same historical ground as its predecessor with many of the same characters, Ralegh among them; it does have the same sort of dense, rich texture of detail, an almost palpable re-creation of things and thoughts, the manners and ways of Elizabethan and Jacobean England. It is another imaginative dreaming of the dream of Adam, the dream of history; but it is also an aesthetic meditation on the creation and revelation of meaning in the succes-

THE SUCCESSION

sion of moments (real, remembered, dreamed, and imagined) that make up the living nexus of time.

Garrett's original intent, as he explains in the prefatory note to the novel, was to follow the success of *Death of the Fox* with another novel, "a tidy and limited task, if not an easy one," to be based on the letters of Elizabeth and James:

It began with the letters—first with the actual letters of Queen Elizabeth (weighty in syntax, knotty in thought, generally obscure in their gnarled tangle of motives) to James IV of Scotland, her godson and cousin and, as it might come to pass, perhaps her heir. His letters, almost always answers and reactions, tend to be more open and obvious to us even though (it seems) he aimed to be sly, canny, clever, forceful, and persuasive. The gist of that story was to be, purely and simply, a narrative accounting of the two of them, Queen and King, exchanging letters over the years, each seeking to come to know and understand the other with a kind of urgent and thorough intimacy that even lovers seldom achieve (vii).

That original plan become lost as Garrett's imagination, engaged in the task of "trying to contemplate two splendid characters," found it needed the help of "ghosts from that time, some of them 'real' (Sir Robert Cecil, Sir Robert Carey, the Earl of Essex) and some of them 'imaginary'—a messenger, a priest, a player, some Scots reivers, etc.

THE ELIZABETHAN NOVELS

And very soon it was clear that if they were to bear witness, they must be allowed to tell their own tales also" (vii-viii). He moved away from an account of the relationship of two people—of necessity, since those two people were a queen and a king—to an account of an entire world, an experiential field in which the realities of the rulers took on substance and meaning and into which their individual identities were subsumed. As Garrett's epigraph (from Arthur Golding's 1567 translation of Ovid's *Metamorphosis*) indicates, the novel itself metamorphosed from the narrative of the interrelationship of two lives into an account of the nature of life itself:

The high, the lowe: the riche, the poore: the mayster, and the slave:
The mayd, the wife: the man, the chyld: the simple and the brave:
The young, the old: the good, the bad: the warriour strong and stout:
The wyse, the foole: the countrie cloyne: the lerned and the lout:
And every other living wight shall in this mirrour see
His whole estate, thoughtes, woordes and deedes expresly shewed to bee.

Having decided to move beyond the concerns of *Death of the Fox*, Garrett had no choice but to

THE SUCCESSION

move beyond its form, to develop a radical form of sufficient complexity to allow him to deal directly with the larger imagination of life itself. When asked by an interviewer about his comment that he had hoped to demonstrate "something about how history happens," Garrett pointed to his method in constructing the book, to his concern with time itself rather than just with remembered time:

I think what I really meant to say there was something about time—something which is more evident in the second novel than in the first, although the first one is involved with memory. The second one has less organized memory than it does [a] kind of simultaneity. In both of them I was trying to deal in different ways with a variety of characters, some of whom don't really cause large things to happen in history but are a part of the whole picture.[20]

The novel has no central character, although Queen Elizabeth and King James are at the center of its events. The succession of its title is certainly that of James to Elizabeth's throne in 1603, but, as Monroe Spears has pointed out, it "is not only that of 1603, but those of 1566, 1587, and 1626."[21] Instead of a central character the novel has many almost unrelated characters—a messenger bearing the news of James's birth to William Cecil, a Catholic priest disguised and on the run, a band of reiv-

THE ELIZABETHAN NOVELS

ers on the Scottish border, an old courtier looking back on the days of his youth, Robert Cecil brooding over and explicating his collection of the letters of Elizabeth and James, a player who was caught up in the rebellion of Essex, a worried King James awaiting word of the old Queen's death, a brooding Queen Elizabeth celebrating her last Christmas, and even a happy drunken plowman walking off his Christmas dinner under the reeling stars.

The novel also has no central time; it shifts in an apparently unordered succession back and forth from 1566 to 1626, not according to the memory of any one character, but according to the experiences and memories and imaginings of all these characters. The brilliance of the novel is not so much that it has so many characters and covers so much time, but that out of all this apparent disorder and disconnection such a coherent and orderly and meaningful whole takes shape. It does not have a modernist preoccupation with fragmentation, but rather a thoroughly postmodernist awareness of interrelatedness and interdependence. By acting so that there is no use in a center, in a completely post-Einsteinian way, Garrett has developed a form in which, even though there is no apparent center, the center holds.

Spears noted the complexity of Garrett's com-

THE SUCCESSION

positional method and his sense of the interdependent nature of what he calls the "imaginary past":

As Garrett says, this is the "imaginary past" in the sense that it has to be imagined—there is no way of automatically reconstructing it (or them, for the past is not one but many, of course) from facts—but it is solidly based on a thorough knowledge of what historical facts and documents are available and, more importantly, of the writings (both literary and personal—e.g., letters) of the period. So this kind of historical novel is a kind of communal product, in a sense: not based on the limited scope of one man's imagination, but on the productions, fictional and real, of many people's minds—a kind of collective reality created by all of them together. . . . It is at the opposite pole from fantasy, where the writer simply unleashes his imagination with no regard for reality or possibility and no constraints. But it is finally dependent on the unifying imagination of a single author.[22]

The philosophical position that gives rise to the complex form of the novel is that things and events, experienced directly or experienced solely imaginatively, are real. An alder leaf falls between two men standing "almost in the shadow of squat old St Cuthbert's Church in Norham village. Sun beginning its summer glide toward twilight, bleeding a faint and wavering reflection of Norham Cas-

THE ELIZABETHAN NOVELS

tle onto the steely-smooth flowing of the Tweed" (34). One of them is the messenger bearing the news of James's birth south to William Cecil; the other is Captain Norton, an old soldier retired in Norham.

A single leaf—waxy green on one side, dusty gray on the bottom, ribbed and shaped like the fat bowl of a lute, floating in motley shade, lighting on the chipped gravel of the footpath, resting briefly between the toes of the four boots of the two of them, then, touched by the merest sigh of a breeze, lifting all at once like a book page to tumble away (35).

Captain Norton studies the leaf. The reader later discovers that the other man, the messenger, is imagining the entire scene in which Norton studies the leaf. The reader knows that George Garrett has imagined the two men, the scene, and the leaf. And yet, there is the leaf, more real to the reader of the novel than any leaf that falls unnoticed in the forest, as real as any leaf that falls noticed or unnoticed in any wood or on any patio or onto and into any fish pond. As real as any page of this book, of any book.

That Essex, for example, does not understand this truth of the imagination—"it was his folly to believe that the Queen had no more substance than the crown and robes she wore. That without

THE SUCCESSION

his eyes to give her life she was diminished to the edge of nothingness" (443-444)—leads him into a solipsistic self-regard that is the source of his failure, morally and politically. Quantum mechanics suggests that the observer affects the thing observed, but it also notes that, despite the blurring of distinctions, the observer is *not* the thing observed and that the reality in which the observer participates has its own integrity and acts on the observer as well. The nature of real experience is much too complex and dynamic for any individual entirely to comprehend, much less to generate singly and sustain in existence.

The key to the formal method of *The Succession*, then, is that meaning is not inherent in any event. Rather, meaning accrues to experience from its relationships in time (past and future and present) and in consciousness, individual *and* shared. To a Christian, the Old Testament became fully meaningful only after it was given meaning by the coming of Christ, but any action that a Christian may now take is fully meaningful only because of Christ's having lived two thousand years ago. The leaf falls; the man notices it; the other man imagines both the leaf and its observer, although the first man is a real man who does live in Norham village. The leaf and the event take on meaning as they are imagined by the character; the

THE ELIZABETHAN NOVELS

leaf and the event and the character take on meaning by their being part of the political events surrounding the birth of Prince James to Mary, Queen of Scots; the leaf, the event, the character, and the birth of Prince James take on meaning thirty-seven years later upon the succession of James to the throne of England; the leaf, the event, the character, the birth of James, and the succession of James take on meaning when imagined and shaped into a novel, *The Succession*, by George Garrett some four hundred years later. And, of course, this actual leaf, the ground reality of this lengthy complex of events, did not even exist until the novel was written, although king and queen and Captain Norton of Norham village and the imagining messenger all did exist centuries before.

The Succession is a novel, a work of the imagination, and as such does not discuss the nature of meaning and its development in the manner of a philosophical text; but its very texture and form allow its readers that rare opportunity, the chance to consider the very nature of experience, to witness and participate in the actual creation of meaning and coherence and order in an apparently meaningless and incoherent and orderless world. Of course, human beings engage in the creation of meaning all the time, but the activity of the committed imagination, the simultaneity of experience

THE SUCCESSION

that it offers, makes them aware of what they are doing, of "how history happens," and gives them the opportunity to understand what they are doing even as they are doing it.

The actual structure of this novel that behaves as though there is no use in a center is still, in one sense, familiarly linear. The reader is expected to read steadily from the beginning of the novel successively to the end, unlike other radically constructed modern novels such as Vladimir Nabokov's *Pale Fire*, Julio Cortázar's *Hopscotch*, or B. S. Johnson's *The Unfortunates*, books which demand of a reader active participation in decisions determining the very order in which pages are to be read. But any reader who expects the 538 pages of *The Succession* to corroborate a "common sense" view of historical process along the steady flight of the arrow of time will be quickly and sorely disappointed. The reader's progress through the sixteen unnumbered sections of the novel may be steady and progressive enough, but the movement of the events in the novel, the imaginative movement through the years between 1566 and 1626, is far from linear, is as radical in conception and execution as any of those more overtly radical novels. "I was hoping I wouldn't be abandoning too many readers," Garrett said. "On the other hand, I couldn't think of any other way to tell this particu-

THE ELIZABETHAN NOVELS

lar story. If I could have, I'd have been delighted to tell it in a straightforward way."[23] Like Umberto Eco, Garrett is counting on the integrity of what he believes to be a necessarily radical form to "produce a new reader," a reader capable of active participation in the openness of the text.

The novel moves from a first section set in March of 1603 back and forth through the succeeding fifteen sections in the following order: 1566, 1603, 1587, 1626 (1575), 1566, 1602, March 1602–1603, 1566, 1626, 1603, 1566, 1602, 1626 (1603), 1566, and finally Christmastide 1602–1603. The story line shifts back forth, too, among a set of characters, most of whom have never met and have no direct connection with each other. Even the two most historically important characters, Queen Elizabeth and King James, never meet but only write letters to each other. And yet all of these characters—the Queen and King, the anonymous messenger, the desperate priest, the band of Scottish reivers, the courtier (Robert Carey, Earl of Monmouth), the actor who has gotten himself tangled up in political intrigue, and Sir Robert Cecil pouring over the letters between Elizabeth and James—function in a vital field of space and time and affect each other directly and indirectly, back and forth, in a dynamic nexus of action, speech,

THE SUCCESSION

memory, dream, and imagination, of transforming and transformative meaning.

Queen Elizabeth, in the first and last sections of the novel, offers the reader both ingress into the book's complexity and egress from it—an Elizabeth near death, looking back over her life, attempting to understand it, to determine its meaning. Her mind wanders, mingling present and past: "And in truth she, too, has lived to become a kind of ghost. Her heart and mind are elsewhere. As if she were exiled to a strange place, a far country she cannot yet name or imagine" (9). She finds herself in her last days, in March of 1603, "moving amid a moving crowd of ghosts. Some of whom are known and named. Named and more or less remembered. Other are like figures from a dream. They are perfect strangers" (10). Like the reader of the novel, she is living in a timeless simultaneity, surrounded by a cloud of ghosts, a web of memory, imagination, and meaning, moving back and forth among known and named figures and perfect strangers. *"Is that how God creates the future?"* Garrett asks in the last section of the novel, a meditative description of the Queen's last (and, therefore, the last Elizabethan) Christmas. *"In the same way that we, who can create nothing out of nothing on our own, constantly seek to recover, repair, and redesign*

THE ELIZABETHAN NOVELS

our past?" (533). The answer to that question may not be answered in any strictly rational manner, and yet the very shape of the book does offer an answer, one of belief and blessing, but one that must be earned by an active involvement in that cloud of ghosts, that web of consciousness which determines all meaning.

The reader, like the old Queen, must listen and remember, note the details of the text, and "recover, repair, and redesign" its varied narratives, forming them (with the complicity of the author) into a meaningful whole. Sir Robert Cecil, in the third section of the novel, "by a wild inspiration" (65) succeeds in hiding from the Queen the dangerous fact that he is receiving letters from James, but the reader knows (and must recover) that the Queen does know of his allegiance all along:

She will hear him out on any subject whatsoever. But without truly listening to him. Certainly without truly believing him. For she knows that his heart and mind are chiefly elsewhere. Are uneasy in attendance in Scotland. For a fact. Heart and mind secretly in service of that man he takes to be most likely to be the King when she is gone (9).

The reader must put those two pieces of information together with other information about Cecil—

THE SUCCESSION

that he is a partner of Ralegh, a man who knows that he must support the right successor in order to survive. It is through Cecil's eyes that the reader gains the opportunity to read the actual letters of Elizabeth and James, and whose interpretations of those letters the reader must trust or disbelieve (in any case, judge) along with his or her own interpretations of them. The meaning of the letters, the thoughts of the character reading the letters, the reader's thoughts about the letters and the character—all of these form the web of meaning which develops in the reading, the experiencing, of the book.

That experience is as richly varied and entertaining as it is complex and intellectually rewarding. The tone is dominated by the old Queen's reveries and is meditative and cloudy with ghosts, but it is no monotone, for the chapters abound with vividly rendered scenes and great liveliness. In the midst of the fourth section, "Priest: 1587," which is composed of the letters and papers of a doomed Catholic priest in hiding and on the run, the single most comic sequence in the novel occurs: an account of the priest and his companion being caught in their disguise as dentists and forced to pull teeth for their very lives. They pull, by accident, the one good tooth in their chief tormentor's mouth, and their only escape is to con-

THE ELIZABETHAN NOVELS

vince the townsmen that the good tooth is the cause of all the bad teeth in the man's mouth:

—It has been proved beyond any question or doubt that the cause of much trouble among teeth is the power and dominion of one great, fat, solid tooth over the others. This tooth—though sometimes there may be more than one, depending on the age, general constitution, and good or ill fortune of the patient—this fat and lordly tooth does set himself up like a hardhearted, arrogant, rack-rent landlord. He does take away the health of the mouth at the expense of the others, his poor tenants, leaving those scranny, shabby fellows nothing but decay and discoloration and grief. He, this great, rich, fat and lordly tooth does grow huge and white like a spoiled ram grazing on common land that has been enclosed and taken away from the people! (84–85)

When, later, this comic priest and teller of the tale is captured and "subjected to considerable rigor" by his captors, only to die "in his sleep sometime during the night after our first session of interrogation" (146), the comedy of his story dissolves in horror, and yet the comedy remains, is as true as his death and is as much a part of the meaning of his life and of its place in the meaning of the larger context of life around him.

Garrett's confidence in his method and his imaginative re-creation of the Elizabethan world

THE SUCCESSION

have advanced to the point that, in this novel, he even dares match himself directly with the primary originator of the historical novel, Sir Walter Scott. In the fifth section, "Courtier: 1626 (1575)," Robert Carey tells of the Queen's famous visit to Kenilworth, the subject (or at least the historical backdrop) of Scott's *Kenilworth*, and in ten pages Garrett summons up "the ghosts of Kenilworth" (166) with sharpness and clarity in a novel that requires none of Scott's romantic interludes and complicated subplots for its excitement. The Kenilworth section does function in the novel beyond its wry tip of the hat to Scott, of course, for it allows Garrett to place Leicester in the nexus of Elizabeth's recollections, along with Ralegh and Essex, whose rebellion appears in the thirteenth section, "Player: 1602."

The reader, then, shares the Queen's memories and thoughts and those of the people around her, reads her and their letters, leaps back and forth in time like an excited researcher, a detective of the historical imagination seeking clues and echoes and nuances that will ultimately create the sense of the whole picture to which the text of the novel gives rise. But this particular "open text" also enforces upon the reader an involvement in the crimes and duplicities of the time beyond that of a detached, even if excited, observer. The mo-

THE ELIZABETHAN NOVELS

ment of electrical imaginative connection in this novel—an equivalent of sorts of the shared letter from Garrett and Ralegh to their sons in *Death of the Fox*—occurs in the thirteenth section when Garrett shifts away from first or third person to a second-person narration; "You have yourself an excellent seat," it opens, "most comfortable bench with a back and a soft, fat embroidered cushion you'd be happy to own" (373). The reader is forced into an identification with an agent "come to London to tie up loose ends in this business of Essex," to cover up any evidence "that your patrons had a genuine interest in the Earl's stratagems" (415). It is in this guise that "you" examine the papers of an actor, looking for signs that he "may have somehow stumbled on more pieces of knowledge than he ought to" (415). "You" find nothing to indicate that he has, but "you" do find out things about "yourself," your imaginatively shared self:

Early you discover he has not. Which is well. For if he had known too much, it might have been necessary to have him killed. Or kill him yourself. Which, either way, by hired hacker or with your own piece of steel, is always troublesome. And which would be a loss, for you took much pleasure from his performance on the stage (415–16).

THE SUCCESSION

Reader and author, intruders in this cloud of ghosts, discover just how deeply an act of committed imagination involves them and unites them with their ghosts, their imagined ancestors, their secret sharers in this fallen and dangerous world, then and now. The use of the second person is a brilliant strategem and is integral to the narrative stance of the entire novel. The world of the Elizabethan succession was, according to Garrett, a world of spies and spying, of lies and lying, duplicitous and deadly and almost staggeringly complex. The reader of this novel is, then, required by the text to become a spy as well, reading over shoulders, listening in on private thoughts, assembling the data, adding them up for private reasons. And in the thirteenth section the reader becomes, by the use of the second person, a player indeed—an actor, a liar, a spy, a killer, a fully human person in a fully human world. And all this by the power of words—words and the committed imagination.

Sir Robert Cecil, reading over the letters of Elizabeth and James, marvels at that power, at the Queen's use of the power of words in her own duplicitous and terribly important game with James:

It could be a subject fit for laughter. How a
wonderfully clever Queen was able to control her

THE ELIZABETHAN NOVELS

young cousin (and all his neighboring northern kingdom) without the use of force of arms. And without fulfilling the usual requirements of large bribes and pensions. Indeed without spending more than the most frugal sums. And how? Chiefly by and through words. Her letters. No small victory in that mastery over a King who is poet and scholar. Defeating him, then, on his own ground and with his own favorite weapons (330).

As the Queen knew, words have great force. They create and they re-create experience and meaning. Words invite readers into the lives of others, allow them to share their victories and fears, their beginnings and their ends. And, perhaps most importantly of all in the work of George Garrett, they allow his readers accommodation with what it is that they are, their humanity and their spiritual identity beyond and through that humanity. What enabled Garrett to write *The Succession* is what enabled Shakespeare or Tolstoy to write at the level they did: a religious belief that gives them an awareness of something larger than the passing moment, that gives them awareness of the presence of the eternal in the temporal, of the universal in the particular, the Word in words.

The time and times of *The Succession* are fully imagined and realized: a world of complexity and

THE SUCCESSION

duplicity, a world of masks and lies and players, a world in which reality and theatricality are inextricably confused, a world of sins and sinners in which the very existence of love seems in question, a world of a virgin queen without issue, a world in which the very future seems in serious doubt. It is a dark world which, as the messenger reminds the reader, is described accurately in scripture: "Child of his times, he finds the truth of Holy Scripture as he reads the story of the world. Who seeks to save his life shall lose it. Who is first now shall be last later. All who have power and influence here and now shall in the end possess no more of either than any beggar lying in a ditch" (20). And yet the succession providentially occurs, the sinful world moves and lives on, and Garrett ends his novel at Christmas, not with the death of the Queen nor even with her recollecting her cloud of ghosts, but with a happy plowman, under the stars, believing himself to be as full of love and charity as he is of "food and drink and gratitude." Garrett allows the reader to share that plowman's belief (and he uses the second person again to assure that sharing), his moment of love and grace in this terrible world:

You believe you are full of love and charity also. And you can wish all the world, your friends and your

THE ELIZABETHAN NOVELS

enemies, nothing but well. Nothing but good fortune. Wishing the dead, from Adam and Eve until now, their rest in peace. And wishing the living, one and all, from the beggar in his hedge to the Queen in her soft bed. . . .
And what is it she can be dreaming of now, as he, half dreaming, imagines her, that lady minted on his hard-earned coins, lady of ballads and prayers in the parish church? Is there a place in her dream for this happy drunken plowman, mud of good English earth thick on his boots, out under the stars, who is wishing for her and the rest of the world, for the sake of our own sweet Jesus, a good night? (538).

This Christian blessing is at the heart of the novel as well as its end; its simplicity informs and gives ultimate meaning to all of the complexity of the novel's radical form. It is not sentimentalized, for the plowman is drunk and only believes himself full of love and charity, and his dream of the Queen has nothing of her dark fears of death in it. It is the other half of the dark Christian truth expressed by the messenger, that the mighty shall be brought low and the "all who have power and influence here and now shall in the end possess no more of either than any beggar lying in a ditch." The dying Queen, brought low by time, and the living plowman blessing her in his cups share in

THE SUCCESSION

the complex Christian description of life in the fallen world of lies that informs this novel. And that blessing is what the reader earns, is the reward for the active participation in the open text of the novel. Not a statement of rational certainty, but one of belief. And that has been the point of *The Succession:* that reality is a complex and vital web (or cloud) of shared perception and consciousness and belief. It is not an account, as most historical novels suggest, of heroes and major figures shaping history for the rest of humankind, but rather of their acting in a nexus of human consciousness, shaped themselves by their human environment even as they shape it. In *The Succession* reality and meaning are one, multiform but ultimately given singular form (a "center") by an intimate relationship with eternity.

Garrett's final meaning may be as old as Christian thought itself, but his radical, postmodern novel gives that meaning new life and new expression. Together with *Death of the Fox, The Succession* stands as a major literary achievement, redefining the very terms of the historical novel and, at the same time, pushing the form of the novel itself into aesthetic *terra incognita,* into the realm of the larger imagination.

THE ELIZABETHAN NOVELS

Notes

1. Monroe K. Spears, "George Garrett and the Historical Novel," *Virginia Quarterly Review* 61 (1985): 262.
2. George Garrett, "Dreaming with Adam: Notes on Imaginary History," *New Literary History* 1 (1969): 420.
3. George Garrett, "Stars Must Fall" (manuscript in the collection of R. H. W. Dillard) 1.
4. Garrett, "Dreaming with Adam" 416.
5. Garrett, "Dreaming with Adam" 413.
6. Garrett, "Dreaming with Adam" 412-16.
7. Garrett, *Death of the Fox* (Garden City: Doubleday, 1971) 10. Further references will be noted parenthetically.
8. Garrett, *The Succession* (Garden City: Doubleday, 1983) viii. Further references will be noted parenthetically.
9. Spears 264.
10. Gertrude Stein, *Narration* (Chicago: University of Chicago Press, 1935) 61.
11. Garrett, "Dreaming with Adam" 419.
12. Jorge Luis Borges, *Dreamtigers* (Austin: University of Texas Press, 1964) 93.
13. Jorge Luis Borges, *Other Inquisitions 1937-1952* (Austin: University of Texas Press, 1964) 78.
14. Garrett, "Stars Must Fall" 2-3.
15. Garrett, "Stars Must Fall" A, 2.
16. Garrett, "Stars Must Fall" A, 1-2.
17. Garrett, "Dreaming with Adam" 420.
18. W. R. Robinson, "Imagining the Individual: George Garrett's *Death of the Fox*," *Hollins Critic* 8 (1971):8-9.
19. Gertrude Stein, *Tender Buttons* (New York: Claire Marie, 1914) 63.
20. "An Interview with George Garrett," *Dictionary of Literary Biography Yearbook: 1983,* ed. Mary Bruccoli and Jean W. Ross (Detroit: Bruccoli Clark / Gale, 1984) 158.
21. Spears 270.
22. Spears 273.
23. "An Interview with George Garrett" 158.

CHAPTER SIX

Poison Pen

In a review of George Garrett's sixth novel, *Poison Pen*, novelist Kit Reed wrote, "This new novel, if that's what it is, by the author of the highly acclaimed *Death of the Fox* and *The Succession*, suggests that behind the elegant facade of the Elizabethan novelist there lurks Bad Georgie, a comic spirit waiting to be unleashed."[1] That *Poison Pen* is the work of "Bad Georgie, a comic spirit" is undeniable, for the novel is a wildly comic, sharply satirical, unkempt rascal of a book, as unlike the enormously disciplined and quietly meditative historical novels as one could imagine. And yet *Poison Pen* is thematically a natural outgrowth of many of the concerns that have given form to Garrett's other novels from *The Finished Man* on, and it also does not stand alone as a solitary comic work in the body of Garrett's fiction.

UNDERSTANDING GEORGE GARRETT

The thematic and formal crux of *The Succession* is a recognition by Garrett that meaning is not a product of the actions of "great men" but is rather the product of the complex interrelationships of the lives of all men. Queen Elizabeth is, in some sense, literally England, not because of her enormous intelligence and the great force of her personality, but because, as queen, she was the point of focus of the vital field that was the English experience. Queens and kings (and political leaders of all kinds) may participate greatly in and even guide the creation of meaning in a society (and ultimately in the world beyond the society in both space and time), but they are not the sole source of that meaning, nor even the primary dynamo of its generation. As Garrett first asserted in *The Finished Man*, each individual member of a society must assume responsibility for its workings, for the nature and behavior of its leaders, for the creation of its meaning.

It is natural enough, given such an understanding of the workings of human society, that the contemporary cult of celebrity should seem to Garrett to be the epitome both of vice and folly and of moral blindness, for it denies that complex and hard-earned truth which has been at the heart of Garrett's "serious" fiction from the very start. And it is also natural enough that a contemporary writer whose sources lie so clearly in Chaucer and whose affinities with the Elizabethans are so strong should find satire to be the appropriate response to the comedy of fools that he sees around him.

As his character and comic alter ego in *Poison Pen*, John Towne, claims to be doing, Garrett too

> is working in the genre of Satire, and he quotes *The Oxford Classical Dictionary* to support himself. He always quotes the general description, to wit that Satire (*Satura*) "may be broadly defined as a piece of verse, or prose mingled with verse, intended to improve society by mocking its anomalies, and marked by spontaneity, topicality, ironic wit, indecent humour, colloquial language, frequent use of dialogue, constant intrusions of the author's personality, and incessant variety in tone and style"[2]

Garrett's satire may be placed, then, as Towne attempts to place his, "in the ancient traditions of Lucilius, of Persius and Juvenal, of Joseph Hall (1574-1656) and his 'byting Satires,' of Pope and Swift and Defoe in *The Shortest Way With Dissenters*" (162).

Long before writing *Poison Pen*, Garrett had exercised the satirical mode in both fiction and poetry. In 1959 he published a group of three comic stories in the *Transatlantic Review* under the title, "3

Fabliaux,"[3] and he has used the term *fabliau* numerous times since to indicate the relationship of his satirical tales to those medieval French verse tales, which were bawdily satirical and were spread across Europe to audiences low and high by traveling *jongleurs*. Stories like the light "Farmer in the Dell"[4] and or the enigmatically dark "And So Love Came to Alfred Zeer"[5] are among the few collected examples of Garrett's modern *fabliaux*, although their satirically comic tone is readily identifiable in other stories and in the novels—especially in Cartwright's sections of *Do, Lord, Remember Me* and in "The Satyr Shall Cry". Garrett began to sound the satirical note early on in his poetry, with the earliest of his skewerings of academic victims appearing in *The Sleeping Gypsy* and he has continued to do so through all of his later collections. Whether he is noting the academic success of the campus nonconformist who gains tenure and promotion despite his "calling on us to rise, rebel, / to shrug the yoke," and who remains "safe in the shadow of his Great Man / a trim Diogenes in a tub of honest tweed"[6], or needling (in "Milksop, the Poetaster") a bad poet who "stared into the mirror on the wall . . . and wrote what isn't poetry at all / to celebrate his bland identity" (95), Garrett's satirical edges are sharp and unmistakable.

POISON PEN

His poems satirizing (and attacking) celebrities are the ones which point most directly to *Poison Pen*. "Celebrity Verses," a set of five poems from the 1960s about media sex goddesses, reveal Garrett's fascination with the powerful allure of these women, or rather with the allure of their photographic images which take on the distorted lives of marionettes in the minds of their male viewers. He finds their sexuality undeniably real, but at the same time discovers that "Ann-Margret can't act," that "Twiggy's a bore," that Kim Novak's "blonder and blander than anyone else," that Barbara Steele "never leaps without a look," and that to touch Donna Michelle "I venture / costs plenty of money" (96–98). The satire of the poems cuts both ways, for even as they reveal the flaws in the women, they confess that nevertheless for the poet the attraction is still there, is still powerful even as its hollowness is revealed: "*Sing hey horny ninny / dong ding and / ding dong.*" The letters in *Poison Pen* to Ursula Andress, Brooke Shields, Cheryl Tiegs, and Christie Brinkley continue to sharpen both edges of the satirical blade of these poems, for there too Garrett satirizes the emptiness of the celebrity subjects but at the same time reveals the complicity of their fans (and the author) in their celebrity and their sham reality.

UNDERSTANDING GEORGE GARRETT

The literary name-games and letters in *Poison Pen* also have their antecedents in the poems. "Flashcards," a set of twenty-one epigrams, gathers many of these barbed literary poems together. There critics and poets are roasted alike in a program which Garrett explains in "Welcome to the Medicine Show":

What I have done here is simply to bottle
some of the natural hatred and malice of poets for
    each other.
I guarantee it will do nothing at all for you.
But it will sure enough shame a hornet or a scorpion.
It can make a rattlesnake laugh and roll over like a
    puppy dog (100).

He expresses his attitude toward a critic, in "To a Certain Critic," by telling of turning over in the woods a rotten log from under which crawls "something very snotlike and pale." He continues, "If it could open its mouth and talk English / you'd know exactly what you sound like to me" (98). Or, in a similar vein, he remembers, in "To a Rival Poet," how after lights out in the barracks

> a hallelujah chorus of farts commenced,
> the least of which was more like music
> and sweeter, too, than any two of yours (99).

POISON PEN

Balancing and complementing these classically satirical assaults on his fellow inhabitants of the literary world are Garrett's self-denigrating poems about his own career and place in that world. "Portrait of the Artist as Cartoon" finds him resolved to embrace "Silence, exile, cunning"

and then the phone rings
and I trip and fall all over myself
running for it, hoping it's for me,
praying my luck has changed, my time has come (99).

And, in "I Must Have Peaked Too Early," he does receive word from the literary establishment, but not in the form he'd hoped:

"Sir, Madame, Person, Occupant,"
the National Endowment addresses me.
"There's still space available and plenty of time
to reserve some of the same for your mortal remains
at the Tomb of the Unknown American Writer" (99).

"Art is long," he confesses, in "Consolations of Philosophy," to Maria Katzenbach, "and I am short" (100). And yet even in these satirical poems of assault and complaint, he does assert the larger realities of the spirit—the beauties of late April or late-night rain, and the hard truth, in "Jacob," that "all angels travel / under assumed names" (102);

and he is able, in "Easter," to pray: "Lord, in your light rising / pray lift my heavy spirit, too" (102).

Poison Pen's fusion of the classical satirical mode of these poems with the broader comedy of the *fabliaux* in a uniquely American manner—the savage slapstick, say, of Mark Twain in *A Connecticut Yankee in King Arthur's Court* with something of the darkness of *The Mysterious Stranger*—was prefigured in the short novel, the religious parody-parable, "The Magic Striptease," which Garrett calls "a comic strip fable."[7] The novella tells the story, including excerpts from his journals, of Jacob Quirk, "the artist of himself" (7), a master mimic who could transform himself into anyone and, eventually, anything: "He decided that people see what they want to see and believe what they care to believe. And this in itself, he ascertained, was at once the strength and the secret of his art" (22). He sees himself, however, not as an actor putting on disguises, but as a nobody hunting for himself, actually taking off identities in a *"hopeless treasure hunt! . . . Call it all a magic striptease. Narcissism raised to the* nth *power!"* (43).

Jacob develops his art and attempts to spread his message, which, as he explains to a disbelieving judge (after he has been arrested for starting a riot at the foot of a statue of Aimee Semple Macpherson while apparently in the guise of Jesus), is

POISON PEN

simply that "in whatever shape and form one finds himself, the one and only possible contentment accessible to a human being is to be at peace with oneself and to rejoice at being alive" (71). Quirk finally decides, having recognized that "the whole world is an asylum for the criminally insane these days" (72), to become the ultimate pop artist—a kind of Andy Warhol of the self—and to transform himself into inanimate objects: "Don't worry about me. Just look for me where you find me" (86). Like a mad modern Walt Whitman (or any artist or prophet), he becomes his book, his journal, which readers may accept or reject or transform as they will:

We can . . . believe the *Journal* if we care to. Or we can believe some parts of it, all the while vehemently denying the truth of other parts. Or we can give a big thumbs down and a fluttering and sloppy Bronx cheer to the whole *bleeping* thing, claiming that, at most, it is just another half-baked example of modern American fiction and about as credible (not more, not less) as, say, *The Warren Report*, or as sincere as the *Tonkin Gulf Resolution*. Or . . . we can safely say that it looks just like the kind of thing that some crazy, misanthropic writer would dream up, the kind of a guy who is so far out of it that he is practically a Quirk himself (88).

And, in fact, at the end of the novella it is suggested to the narrator by the Bishop of one of many schismatic Protean churches which follow Quirk as Master that the missing Quirk may perhaps "turn into this book you are writing" (107). And, as the Bishop adds, "Why not?"

Garrett—or Quirk, or the unnamed narrator—takes Quirk's refined art as the occasion for satirical jabs at modern life: at politics, at publishing, at psychology and show business, at the cult of celebrity in general. For example, Dr. Smartheim, the German psychiatrist who "argues, most persuasively," that the 1940s "never really happened, in his brilliant contribution to revisionist history—*The Lost Decade of the Forties: A Study in Mass Hallucination*"—decides that his study of Quirk "is a preliminary indication, initial evidence of a plausible hypothesis that a great many public figures are only mass hallucinations, the products of the corrupt and decadent mass consciousness of our times" (89–90). Ridiculous as he may be, his conclusion is not one that Quirk or Garrett would find implausible. The meaning of reality is at best the creation of those who are sharing in its life, and the cheapening of the contemporary imagination—an imagination not grounded in a belief larger than itself—leads to a cheapened and even hallucinatory reality.

Garrett does not leave his parable with that bleak conclusion, but rather, as he did in the satiri-

POISON PEN

cal poems, he turns the satire on himself and also indicates a meaning to life larger than the vice and folly which seems to define it. Quirk turns himself into the clock of his agent, who calls himself Irving Schmertz. The elaborate clock with a Crusader and a Saracen who smite each other on the hour is, as any reader of Garrett's *Death of the Fox* would recognize, Sir Francis Bacon's clock, which figures in an important scene in that serious novel.[8] In "The Magic Striptease," however, the clock becomes another of Quirk's assaults on modern folly, with the Saracen killing the Crusader and shouting, "Black Power, you Mother-*blanker!*" and with "all kinds of other figures . . . instead of the knights, usually in pairs and up to no good whatsoever" (101). The scene in the novella could be read as further commentary on the vanity of Bacon's very human wishes, but it must also be seen as evidence that Garrett knows not to take his own serious work too seriously.

The indication of a meaning to life larger than that of the fallen world of lies may be found in Quirk's own message: his satirical popping of the pretensions around him, and his belief that "the only thing worth doing, in the brief wink of light that we call a lifetime, is to learn again and again to suffer and to rejoice" (59). The tone of Quirk's explaining his decision that God is fair—"I want

Him to understand that I am ready to forgive Him for everything, if He'll do the same for me" (77)—is reflected in that of the novella's epigraph, a line by the comedian Brother Dave Gardner: "Gratitude is riches and complaint is poverty and the worst I ever had was wonderful." "Bad Georgie's" lesson turns out to be in keeping with those of the serious author of the meditative historical novels, and the comic tone does not negate the seriousness of Garrett's point: that in this fallen world of lies, redeemed only by divine sacrifice and atonement, "the only thing worth doing" *is*, in the fullest sense, "to learn again and again to suffer and to rejoice."

Poison Pen extends that understanding and the comic method of "The Magic Striptease" and the other satirical poems and stories into complicated new ground, rendering as it does a fiercely comic social history of America during the twenty years of its composition, from the mid-1960s through the mid-1980s. The account of the novel's composition is even more complicated than that of *Do, Lord, Remember Me*, for it too has risen from the ruins of a much larger work, a genuine *roman maudit*, *Life With Kim Novak Is Hell*. Parts of that novel have been appearing in magazines for years: poison pen letters to celebrities by Garrett's alter ego character, the truly reprehensible John Towne; "Jane Amor,

POISON PEN

Space Nurse,"[9] one of Towne's many plans for novels; and even the at once ridiculously comic and powerfully moving story "A Record as Long as Your Arm,"[10] formed of the original beginning and end sections of the huge work, contains the ghost of the lost novel. In the opening section of *Poison Pen*, "*Psst . . . a little preface,*" Garrett claims that Towne is the actual author of the novel but also that he is a character in the larger novel (and, later, that he is the author of that novel, too), and he offers at least a brief glimpse of the nature of the larger work:

All that follows was written by John Towne. Who is really a *character*. I mean that literally. He is really and only a character in a novel that I *am* writing and have been working on, off and on, since the early 1960s. The novel was/is called *Life With Kim Novak Is Hell*. Which is not a fact or even a reasonable supposition, but a headline from *The National Enquirer*. Which is just the sort of tacky and trashy publication that John Towne tends (almost always) to read instead of important and intelligent and uplifting stuff like the fiction of John Updike or, say, the serious poetry of Mark Strand. . . . Unfortunately his half-assed *style* seems to have had some pernicious influence on me, as well as on other characters in *Life With Kim Novak Is Hell*. At least my friends say so. They say that at times, *stylistically,* you can't tell us apart. Content-wise, however, we are worlds apart (x).

UNDERSTANDING GEORGE GARRETT

He goes on to say that the recent poison pen letters in the book would seem to indicate that Towne is back again:

In a way I hope that he is not back among us. For if he is, then I may yet have to finish *Life With Kim Novak Is Hell*, if only to be rid of him for good and all.

Of course, chances are that no self-respecting American publisher, large or small, would ever publish that novel. I certainly hope not. As values and standards all around us crumble like Hostess Twinkies in the grubby little fists of children raised on Wonder Bread and Captain Kangaroo, it is reassuring to know that the American publishing business remains what it has always been—a serious, if not especially profitable industry devoted to long boozy lunch hours and to the ceaseless search for . . . well, for lack of a better word, *quality*.

(Try not to get any of that quality on your shoes. It is hard to get off. And it stinks.) (x–xi)

It seems likely, then, that *Poison Pen* is itself the only version of *Life With Kim Novak Is Hell* that Garrett is ever likely to publish: only the wildly satirical parts of the larger work, with the long letter from Garrett to Christie Brinkley (which the reader is asked not to read) standing in place of the original "serious" ending (which now concludes the story "A Record as Long as Your Arm").

POISON PEN

Poison Pen is certainly rich enough and complex enough to stand on its own as an important work, as well as to stand in for its large, lost parent work. It is an elaborately self-contradictory work, and that self-contradiction is essential to its structure. It is fiercely satirical and savagely anarchistic in its values, even while it is quietly and seriously humane and Christian. It is irrealistic, openly artificial, and parodic of traditional "realistic" fiction, even while it is as parodic of artificial, irrealistic fiction. It is so apparently right-wing in many of its political assaults that Thomas Fleming praised its "reactionary social vision" and called it "nothing short of the most powerful satire on American life and letters, not just since Mencken and Twain, but *ever.*"[11] At the same time its assaults on many of the idols of the American right wing led Clyde Wilson to note that in addition to its attacks on the liberal establishment it "bashes Goldwater and Reagan, the FBI and the IRS, fundamentalists and the corporate culture."[12] It is so vulgar in what it says and the way that it says it, even while it is seriously moral and aesthetically complex, that it led Fleming to say, "The only writer who combines the same loftiness of purpose with anything like this vulgarity of speech is Aristophanes. Rabelais doesn't even come close."[13]

Those kinds of internal contradictions are reflected in the novel's structure. It is ostensibly a collection of the abandoned papers and letters of John Towne, an academic gypsy and literary con man, edited by an assistant professor of English, Lee Holmes, who is hustling for unlikely tenure, and

> if he doesn't publish something (anything) somewhere, and pretty quick too, he is flat finished as far as his career is concerned as the oldest Assistant Professor at the small woman's college in southwest Virginia, . . . which Holmes, out of fear as much as any innate sense of decency and decorum, insists on calling Nameless College (5).

The task was also forced on Holmes as a means of repaying a publisher for an advance on a novel "to be freely adapted from the romantic, truelife adventures of Gabriele D'Annunzio and Eleanora Duse. When Holmes couldn't or wouldn't write that book he had contracted to do, the publisher 'allowed' him to pay off the advance by editing the papers of the aforesaid Towne" (38). Fraud, in other words, compounds itself in the world of *Poison Pen*, and this Holmes, even though he seeks to discover the truth of the puzzle of John Towne, is no Sherlock (and no true namesake of the honorable Southern hero, Lee, either). By the end of the

POISON PEN

novel he has, after twenty years, finished the task as best he can and has at least attained the dubious title of "Assistant Professor Emeritus" (212) at Nameless College. But he also appends a lonely and pathetic note to the novel which reveals that not every fraud comes out smelling like a rose: "If any of you are former students of mine at Nameless, I wouldn't mind hearing from you time to time. Even a postcard can make my day these days" (214).

John Towne, in this novel, if not in "A Record as Long as Your Arm," is unflappable and unstoppable, in full thorny bloom at beginning and end. Whether he is conning himself into print or into the bedrooms of the wives of his colleagues; whether he is writing an advice column as "Dr. Wisdom" for a sleazy magazine published by Totem Pole Press; or whether he is hustling his way through England in the guise of a Negro clergyman named Radio P. King, he is more like a natural force than a possibly ordinary, possibly redeemable human being: something like a tornado or a plague of locusts. He explodes on a scene with much the same impact as the external forces that transform the small southern towns in the *Do, Lord, Remember Me* tryptich. He has literary antecedents throughout the history of literature—characters like the fast-talking con men who populate the fiction of Mark Twain—but two more recent ones seem particularly important: the devilish preacher Semon Dye in Erskine Caldwell's *Journeyman* and, especially, the villain of one of Garrett's favorite novels, Calder Willingham's *Eternal Fire*, the demonic Harry Diadem. John Towne may lack the relentless force of those two characters, and he certainly does not meet the amazingly violent end that Harry Diadem does, but he is at least their cousin, an operator and manipulator, completely amoral, a user and abuser of women, a total sham, and a remarkably clear lens through which to examine the sham and hypocrisy in the immoral fallen world of lies around him.

John Towne also functions as a clownish and grotesque parody of Garrett himself, and he allows Garrett thereby to examine once again the double nature of human beings—the sinner-saint, the suffering rejoicer, the redeemed fallen man—with a new freedom. By setting Towne (and "Bad Georgie") free to say and do what they will, to let vice and folly (to say nothing of copulation) thrive, Garrett enables himself to satirize the contemporary world without restraint and, at the same time, finds a formal unity which will place that satirical wildness in a meaningful aesthetic and moral structure. Towne is, then, a distorted mirror image of Garrett: both are former soldiers, college profes-

POISON PEN

sors, novelists, Hollywood script writers, and authors of an unpublished novel called *Life With Kim Novak Is Hell;* and, in the pages of this book, both become practically indistinguishable, with the reader left uncertain which voice he or she is hearing at any given time. But lest readers become hopelessly confused and decide that Garrett and Towne are identical, Garrett reminds them in the last long section of the novel, "A Very Personal and Private Letter" (a section which, by the way, readers are requested not to read), that Garrett has actually done (and successfully) all the important things that Towne has only attempted or claimed to have done (written novels and films, had an academic career), and that Garrett has a human reality beyond the pages of the book (or any book), and that this reality—for all the fact that like his fellow humans he is an imperfect man leading an imperfect life in an imperfect world—is the one true ground from which all meaning in a chaotic and absurd world must spring.

Towne has, as far as the reader can ascertain, actually written and published books; he is, for example, the purported author of his first novel, *Live Now & Pay Later* (the title of which also serves as the subtitle of *Poison Pen*), but he later "admits that it was 'freely adapted from' an unpublished manuscript entitled 'A Home for Reckless Spenders,' by Ray Wadley" (27), whose wife Towne also stole. For Totem Pole Press he also claims to have written a Hollywood novel called *Goldwyn Boy* and a novelization of his own script for "a low budget 'nudie' film" called *Mondo Teeny Boppo* (29); he also mentions another novel called *Last of the Big Time Spenders* (55), which may or may not be indebted to Wadley's manuscript. He suggests that if he were a "Big Shot . . . Pop Philosopher with an ax to grind and metaphorical heads to cut off" (72), he would write a book called *The Triumph of Shinola; or, My Country and Whatever Became of It?* In a long letter to his agent, Sam, he proposes writing a "*Serious Novel*" (55) to be called *The Realms of Gold;* this unwritten novel features a character named R. C. Alger, "the last direct descendant of Horatio Alger" (58), a bedridden sufferer from a degenerative disease who fills his time working on two projects: "a major, documented work of history entitled 'America the *Beautiful?:* From Pioneers to Pansies' " (60) and an elaborate series of bitter and cynical poison pen letters to celebrities, the actual authorship of which is always carefully concealed.

Selections from the fictive letters of the fictional Alger (a character in a proposed fiction by the fictional John Towne) constitute a large portion of Garrett's *Poison Pen* and provide the title. Like

POISON PEN

Guy Grand, "the last of the big spenders," in Terry Southern's novel *The Magic Christian*, Alger goes to great effort and expense because of his "very unusual attitude toward *people*; . . . as he expressed it himself, '*making it hot for them.*' "[14] Garrett takes full advantage of the layers of fiction surrounding Alger's letters to launch his satirical attacks on America the less-than-beautiful and especially on its "Beautiful People." Among the many targets of the letters are politicians (Lyndon Johnson, Barry Goldwater, Robert Kennedy, George Wallace, Jimmy Carter, Teddy Kennedy, Ronald Reagan, and others); other public figures (Bishop Pike, Livingston Biddle, James Farmer, sex therapists Masters and Johnson, Hugh Hefner, Truman Capote, Mrs. John DeLorean, and others), and the "sex goddesses" of two decades (Ursula Andress, Jean Shrimpton, Linda Lovelace, Brooke Shields, and Cheryl Tiegs). The tone of all the letters is that of professed innocence and vulgar honesty. The letter to Ronald Reagan, for example, deals with his looks: "You really look terrific these days. Who does your hair? Who is your Makeup Person? I, myself, am a Mortician by trade, and I can tell a really good job when I see one" (163). A drunken, thoroughly racist and sexist, but apparently sincere Princeton alumnus offers Brooke Shields advice on life as an Ivy Leaguer, with reference to the problems of Jody Foster: "You didn't know Hinckley, too, did you?" (173). A spastic admirer of the Playboy Philosophy writes to Hugh Hefner demanding some action: a Bunny, in fact (86–91). Garrett thoroughly covers the full range of morally vulnerable American public life, transforming bad taste into an effective scalpel in the great satiric tradition.

The metafictional structure and texture of the novel, which calls attention to the surface of the text as in no other Garrett novel, forces both the amused and the offended reader to test his or her assumptions about the relationship of a fictional text to the real world, and ultimately to consider the amount of fiction which is inescapably part and parcel of that reality. Another great artistic examiner of the fictive nature of the real and one of Garrett's favorite film directors, Federico Fellini, said, "I see no dividing line between imagination and reality."[15] Like Fellini, Garrett explores the interrelationship of the fictive and the real in *Poison Pen* and finds a world in which both the truths and the self-serving lies of the fallen world and the true lies of fiction generate and illuminate each other, achieve meaning beyond the limitations of each in their vital interchange.

George Garrett the author intrudes frequently and blatantly into the fictional texts (and fictive

POISON PEN

layers of text) in *Poison Pen*, claiming that Professor Wayne C. Booth's critical theories make it "safe to say that it is perfectly all right and not even considered bad manners any more for an author to *intrude*" (37). He comments on Towne and Towne's fictions, and on the novel and its structure. He even includes a letter from himself to publisher Gordon Lish, suggesting that Lish's novel *Dear Mr. Capote* found its source in one of Towne-Alger's poison pen letters (to Capote) which Lish had asked to consider for publication in *Esquire* in 1970: "And if you need any little teeny-tiny nudge to get started on your next novel, please feel free, indeed feel *welcome*, to use anything of mine you want to. We are all in this together, Gordon, and people should be more helpful to each other. At least that's the way I feel about it. How do you feel?" (104).

The largest and most significant authorial intrusion into the fictional text, however, the one which draws the interplay of the fictive and real into sharp focus and gives thematic unity to the apparently chaotic metafictional text, is the long letter from Garrett to model (and ultimate sex symbol of the 1980s) Christie Brinkley which concludes the novel (with the exception of one last intrusion of his own by Towne). This long letter includes a complete copy of Garrett's academic vita and an account of his receiving his doctoral degree at Princeton thirty years after he finished all the requirements except the dissertation when "some emeritus professors decided that my two historical novels, *Death of the Fox* and *The Succession,* could qualify as a dissertation" (225), and an ironic account of his being warned by his employers at the University of Virginia in the 1960s that he should not waste his time working on a novel (*Death of the Fox*) but should finish his dissertation!

The letter continues from its account of Garrett's professional (and public) life to discuss his vision of the essential and pervasive dishonesty of the public life of the fallen world: "If all the Leaders, all the Celebrated and the Celebrities in the U.S.A. in every field of endeavor were subjected to a Phonus Balonus Test or, in lieu of that, a simple Lie Detector Test, I am persuaded beyond the least shadow, thin as a single blade of grass, of doubt that there is not one among them who could pass" (233). In this world it is not difficult to understand, he concludes, that for ordinary people, "for all of us, Celebrities and Public Figures are not *Real People*" (236):

Ergo: "What happens to them, doesn't really happen to anyone. It is all just part of an on-going fable or fairy tale in which they (the Celebrities or Public

POISON PEN

Figures) are trapped or imprisoned. They are there by choice, of course, having accepted their essential unreality along with their first fame and first fat pay checks. People don't mean any harm, Christie. They just don't take Celebrities very seriously. Or, to put it in another way, they take them very seriously indeed (sometimes), but never in fact and flesh, only in fiction and fantasy" (236).

Garrett goes on to talk to the essentially unreal celebrity Brinkley as though she were quite real, to satirize her public self and that of her public husband Billy Joel, to admit that he has "your splendid poster and colorful calendars making a mockery of their two dimensions on my attic wall" (257), but also to wish her well—and to satirize his wishing well a person who is really only a sexual fantasy and fiction to him:

Stay well, Christie.
Have a nice private life.
Take good care of your privates.
Lord bless you and keep you. Lord lift up his
countenance upon you. Etc. . . .
Love XXX
The Author

Garrett is quite aware in those concluding lines that it is George Garrett the author talking to Christie Brinkley the character in the letter, and that George Garrett the private person is only very distantly (and only through the medium of a fictive text and its countless readers) talking to Christie Brinkley the private person at all. He wishes her "a nice private life" even as he satirizes the overt and available sexuality of her public self.

The key to the novel—the moral ground of its harsh satire and the reason for its complex metafictional form—is Garrett's understanding that a distinction must be made between real private lives and fictional public ones if any kind of sanity is to be secured in the fallen world of lies. There may be no dividing line between imagination and reality, as Fellini suggested, but a dividing line must nevertheless be maintained between private and public life, between real human beings and the plethora of illusory images of human beings with which we are constantly surrounded, between a saint and what Gertrude Stein called "a publicity saint."[16] Garrett allows a real woman (his wife, Susan) to explain to a fictional woman (Christie Brinkley) and to himself the point of the book:

My wife said to me, simply: "Public life is an illusion. Only private life is real and matters." I expect she is right. I expect that is the theme of this letter. I expect, also, that it is the subtext, the hidden theme and true

POISON PEN

subject of all of Towne's work. Thus it is the major theme of *Poison Pen* and, as well, of the larger work (unfinished and unpublished)—*Life With Kim Novak Is Hell*, from which *Poison Pen* is excerpted (257).

At the end of the story "A Record as Long as your Arm," John Towne, who has addressed the whole story to Ray Wadley, whose wife he has stolen (if only temporarily), reveals that Ray has killed himself. The ludicrously comic tale of adultery becomes deadly serious, and the necessity for treating other people as real people and not just as fictions necessary to our own needs becomes painfully clear. Towne does not ask Ray's forgiveness ("The dead do not care anymore") and seems to be trying to dodge his own guilt and responsibility, but then he quite unexpectedly expresses the truth of Garrett's world as clearly as it has ever been expressed:

Not that people can ever completely forgive each other. But in the ritual of wishing to and trying to forgive one another, in ceasing to judge one another and leaving Judgment to its proper Author, then for a brief moment we can find and feel the secret energy of divinity within us.
Forgiveness is a simple and glorious act of human freedom. Suicide and lunacy are not. Sartre and

UNDERSTANDING GEORGE GARRETT

Camus were full of shit.
You think I'm too serious all of a sudden? Well, you're right, old buddy. Right about that anyway.[17]

Towne, the sinner and con man, gets the last serious and even profound word in the story and in the novel *Life With Kim Novak Is Hell*, and the reader of the story can at least sense in that richly ironic and ambiguous ending something of the complexity of that much larger work.

Garrett does the job for himself in *Poison Pen*, establishing a real world of friends and private lives in the Christie Brinkley letter that gives the lie even more fully to the pretensions of that public (and publicity) world that means too much to us all. Towne does slip in on the last page of the novel (with an alphabet of names of celebrities who do not appear in the novel—but now, of course, do) as a warning that Jack Towne may finally have the last word in more ways than one; but he does not manage to dissipate the profundity and emotional seriousness of the Brinkley letter. "Bad Georgie" gives way, as he must, to the serious author, and *Poison Pen* joins the body of Garrett's serious work rightfully and, with a clown's healthy irreverence, significantly. It, like its predecessors, *Death of the Fox* and *The Succession*, continues Garrett's exploration into human meaning and into expressive liter-

POISON PEN

ary form, an exploration that gives no signs of being even near an end.

Notes

1. Kit Reed, "A Menagerie of Letters," *The Hartford Courier* 15 June 1986: G3.

2. George Garrett, *Poison Pen; or, Live Now and Pay Later* (Winston-Salem, NC: Stuart Wright, 1986) 162. Further references will be noted parenthetically.

3. Garrett, "Three Fabliaux," *Transatlantic Review* 1 (1959): 106-27.

4. Garrett, *An Evening Performance* (Garden City: Doubleday, 1985) 220-26.

5. Garrett, *A Wreath for Garibaldi* (London: Rupert Hart-Davis, 1969) 100-08.

6. "Gadfly," *The Collected Poems of George Garrett* (Fayetteville: University of Arkansas Press, 1984) 90-91. Further references will be noted parenthetically.

7. Garrett, *The Magic Striptease* (Garden City: Doubleday, 1973). Further references will be noted parenthetically.

8. Garrett, *Death of the Fox* (Garden City: Doubleday, 1971) 499.

9. Garrett, "Jane Amor, Space Nurse," *Fly By Night* 1 (1970) 47-57.

10. Garrett, *An Evening Performance* 444-66.

11. Thomas Fleming, "Free Adaptations," *The National Review* 7 Nov. 1987: 53-54.

12. Clyde Wilson, "Literature and Manners," *Book World* 10 (1987): 410.

13. Fleming 53.

14. Terry Southern, *The Magic Christian* (New York: Random House, 1960) 10.

15. Federico Fellini, *Fellini on Fellini* (New York: Delacorte / Seymour Lawrence, 1976) 152.

16. Donald Sutherland, *Gertrude Stein: A Biography of Her Work* (New Haven: Yale University Press, 1951) 154.

17. Garrett, *An Evening Performance* 466.

CHAPTER SEVEN

Poems and Short Stories

It is difficult to describe the wide range of George Garrett's writing beyond the novels, for he has written a large body of poems, stories, plays, screenplays, scholarly articles, critical articles, and essays. His critical and biographical study *James Jones*, for example, is a book that is important not only for its insights into Jones and his work, but also for its analysis of the American experience during and after World War II, a time that "can be understood not merely as a time of transition or of gradual transformation of society, but as a time of the most complex and radical changes."[1] Therefore it is a book that moves well beyond the immediate demands of its subject to enrich its reader's understanding of the vital context of fact and idea which surrounds and informs the subject. Garrett's other scholarly and critical work (on William Faulkner, Joyce Cary, James

Gould Cozzens, F. Scott Fitzgerald, and Robert Penn Warren, among others; on American WASP humor, contemporary poetry and fiction, and the literary and publishing scene) is remarkable for that same ability to place the subject in its broadest context and to shed significant light on both that subject and the context.

Garrett's plays do not constitute a major body of work, but they too exhibit the variety of his interests and the range of his skills and talent. *Sir Slob and the Princess* is a play for children, and, as its title suggests, is a modern variant on a familiar fairy tale situation. It is, with its delightfully direct storytelling, another example along with many of his short stories of the strong influence on Garrett's work of the medieval *fabliau*. *Garden Spot, U.S.A.*, a two-act comedy, was produced at the Alley Theatre in Houston in 1962; in its satirical view of a buzzard-plagued town which comes to thrive and depend on the presence of the birds for tourists and the money they bring, it is a clear precursor of the kind of sharp-edged humor which was to mark Garrett's later fiction, the *Do, Lord, Remember Me* tryptich and *Poison Pen*. *Enchanted Ground* was written for a celebration of the eightieth anniversary of the Old Gaol Museum in York, Maine (near Garrett's home for many years in York Harbor) and is a play, both in subject matter and in

POEMS AND SHORT STORIES

narrative technique, closely akin to *Death of the Fox* and *The Succession*. In it a man and a woman, speaking for many others over the centuries, weave the past together with the present to form a verbal tapestry of meaning, ghosts speaking to living beings, "no more substantial than shadows, . . . lighthearted shadows, . . . a cloud of witnesses . . . who wish you only well."[2] Like the concluding section of *The Succession* (which was published separately in 1979 as *To Recollect a Cloud of Ghosts*), the play attempts a reconciliation of alien past and the present by the force of the committed imagination in shared belief and good will.

The film scripts of George Garrett also relate to and exhibit the same variety as his major work, although the necessities of working in a collaborative medium where a director has the final say make them less immediately *his* work. *The Young Lovers*, directed by Samuel Goldwyn, Jr., is a film about college students and their problems at the very beginning of the Vietnam War. The ambiguity of its open ending, its use of a set of visual symbols to support and give meaning to the plot, and especially its complex of intertextual allusions to earlier films give it value far beyond its basic story. *The Playground*, an independent film directed by Richard Hilliard, extends and develops the formal innovations of the Hollywood film, using actors in multiple roles and reflexively breaking the "fourth wall" by bringing the film makers and the making of the film into the story and onto the screen. A comedy about death, the film parodies familiar attitudes about death and cinematic conventions in the presentation of those attitudes; its healthy Christian laughter, which is also directed at clichés of Christian belief and behavior, functions as a remarkable anodyne for the very genuine pain and fear of death in the film. It certainly deserves more attention than it ever received.

Garrett's other produced film script, coauthored with two of his colleagues at the University of Virginia, deserves the attention it has received, but in a very different way. Written with tongue in cheek and listed by Harry and Michael Medved as one of "the worst movies ever made,"[3] *Frankenstein Meets the Space Monster* is a parody of cheap science fiction films while managing to be one itself. Certain scenes in it (an abduction of a bathing beauty on a beach by spacemen while her portly companion reads his newspaper, General Bowers's reading the funny papers in the midst of an invasion from another planet) have the satirical and low comic feel of *Poison Pen*.

All of Garrett's work deserves close and careful critical attention, for it is all very much of a

POEMS AND SHORT STORIES

piece, with a unity of vision and a developing and evolving craft despite its great variety. But it is the large and important body of poetry and short fiction which remains undeniably necessary to an understanding of his work. As David R. Slavitt has pointed out, Garrett "has had less recognition for his poetry and short fiction than he might have received had he not been a novelist, or anyway not such an extraordinarily good one,"[4] but if he had never written the novels, these poems and stories would still earn him a significant place in American literary history.

The Poems

Writing of *The Reverend Ghost*, a book which he had selected for the Scribner's "Poets of Today" series, John Hall Wheelock found George Garrett to be "a poet fascinated, and even tormented, by what might be termed the essence of things, those inner presences which, though unapparent and wearing the mask of object or event, make object and event what they are."[5] The poems, both those in that initial collection and those that followed, as Wheelock recognized, are parabolic and enigmatic in nature, written from Garrett's vision of the double nature of human beings (sinners and saints, fallen and redeemed) and of the double nature of life itself (its meaning growing from fact, its meaning incarnated in fact). They are grounded in everyday experience, but they are never merely anecdotal; they press always toward human and metaphysical meaning, toward the truth that may still be found (or formed) in the desert of contemporary experience.

Garrett is a poet of the postwar years, the disillusioned years of the continuing cold war. "It is hard," he says in *James Jones*, "for those who lived through it to remember back before World War II, to recall that world so different that it might have been dreamed or only visited, like a foreign country."[6] He strives in his poems to understand that lost world of heroism and faith, the traditional realm of poetry, and to accommodate it to this age of anxiety, shattered hopes, and pandemic phobias. His poetry records a personal journey through the army and a time in Rome, his years in school and after, the transformation of his love into a growing family, and his growing recognition of his frailty and mortality in a world in which everything tastes of death and where every skull grins a lewd secret. It is a dark and Augustinian journey, fraught with doubts and terrors, lighted by love and his Christian faith, made bearable (and made

POEMS AND SHORT STORIES

into poetry) by his intelligence and the strength of his imagination.

In the poem "For a Bitter Season" he describes the darkness within himself and in the world around him, as he thinks at night of the dying oak tree in his yard:

> Now I am a stranger and my oak tree dies
> young. Blight without a name, a bad omen.
> I die, too, fret in my familiar flesh,
>
> and I take this for a bitter season.
> We have lived too long with fear. We take
> fear for granted like a drunken uncle,
>
> like a cousin not quite all there
> who's always there. I have lived too long
> with the stranger who haunts my mirror.

Finally, thinking of his family and the baby daughter born the spring before, he utters a prayer, itself the only answer in a bitter season:

> Bless us, a houseful of loving strangers,
> one good woman, too small boys, a man
> waking from sleep to cough his name.
>
> And bless my daughter made of snow and bluest
>   eyes.[7]

Garrett's intensely personal poems constitute only one of many strands in the tapestry of his poetry. He has written witty, satirical poems ("From the Academy," "Three Characters in Search of a New Dunciad," "Celebrity Verses," "Flashcards"); he has evoked the moods and essences of real places ("In Tuscany," "Percé Rock," "Old Slavemarket: St. Augustine, Fla.," "Crows at Paestum," "Maine Weathers"); he has written poems which approach literary figures with telling insight ("Congreve," "Matthew Arnold," "Caedmon," "General Prologue," "Swift"); he has re-created larger figures from a real and mythic past ("Tiresias," "Eve," "Abraham's Knife," "Salome"), and he has written striking love poems of an almost seventeenth-century complexity and force ("Some Women," "Shards for Her," "Invitation," "Since It Is Valentine's Day"). The variety seen in even this brief list offers evidence of the vitality of Garrett's poetic imagination; and that vitality, along with his technical skill, gives the poems, for all their variety, a genuine unity of vision and manner.

Garrett's poems have a clearly identifiable sound. The early poems, which Wheelock found "bare yet often strangely musical" and often "curiously abstract,"[8] are tightly formal, intellectually taut, and almost explosively condensed; but his later poems, without losing that tension even in open forms, achieve a working fusion of the heightened diction of poetic meditation and the

POEMS AND SHORT STORIES

fresh and exciting immediacy of colloquial speech. In an early poem about spring ("The March Problem"), "The wind became a green idea" (103) in strictly controlled iambic tetrameter quatrains, but in a later one ("Forsythia") spring erupts in appropriately ragged and unkempt language and lines:

> Yellow plain yellow
> everywhere common
> sometimes neat & soft
> as a puff of smoke
> more often unkempt
> extravagant & formless
> barbaric & blatant (50).

In "Meditations on Romans," Garrett makes the universal particular in a very real present of nails and dollar bills and in a language as ordinary as the objects it names and as new and clean as its juxtapositions are unexpected and startling. It is a poem of spiritual doubt and desire made real in words and images of this world, just as soul lives in dying flesh. The poem concludes:

Christ, prince and physician, carpenter, king,
come shining as a new nail in my waking dream
when (as ever shall be) skin and bones
go slack and even fresh air is a bad taste,
when thoughts are soiled as dollar bills
and soul is no more than a hat on a shelf.

UNDERSTANDING GEORGE GARRETT

> Come then, I pray, to play on my nerves
> a new song. Of my bones make piano keys
> and of my thoughts make clouds of birds,
> dark impulses fleeing from the cold.
> Yoke my shrugging shoulders, set upon my soul
> (Thy will be done) the brightest crown of thorns.[9]

Whether Garrett is laughing with or at the world, celebrating its delights beyond our most just deserts, speaking intimately and intensely, or just bravely pressing on in the face of a harsh and bitter season,

> I straighten my tie and grit my teeth
> in what I hope and trust will pass
> for a polite, uncertain grin ("Rugby Road" 68)

his language maintains its distinctive vigor, its honest and thoroughly American use of the vernacular for the most noble and complex of purposes.

His version of an epigraph by Martial stands as an honest (and very self-deprecating) introduction to his work, as well as a typical use of his distinctive language:

> To the reader: when you look
> inside, you're bound to find here
> some good verses, some middling, and I fear
> plenty of bad ones. What can I say?

POEMS AND SHORT STORIES

> Buddy, it's the only way
> a poet can make a book (102).

The book George Garrett made contains far more good verses than middling or bad, and many poems that seem undeniably major works (especially "Abraham's Knife," "Salome," "Luck's Shining Child," "Meditations on Romans," "Maine Weathers," "Rugby Road," "Fig Leaves," "For My Sons," "Out on the Circuit," and "Some Women"), poems that in craft and art stand out in their time, and help to define each reader's own time as they linger and grow in the mind.

The Short Stories

Just as George Garrett's poetry has moved toward more open diction and form, so his short fiction has developed too, from traditionally realistic stories, strongly influenced by Hemingway and Faulkner, toward increasingly more enigmatic and parabolic stories, "open texts." Even the structure of his first collection of stories, *King of the Mountain*, prefigures the shape of that development. The opening story, "The Rivals"—the story of a boy's coming of age and to terms with his unrecognized rivalry with his father as they both face their mutual rival, the ocean—is, for all its richness and emotional complexity, a traditionally constructed and written story. But the concluding piece, "What's the Purpose of the Bayonet?" is a group of five stories about Army life, varying in tone and style, almost anecdotal, and requiring the reader's active participation as coadjutor in the creation of its overall form and meaning.

The body of Garrett's short fiction is large; he estimates in the preface to *An Evening Performance* that the thirty-eight stories in that 518-page collection make up "a little less than half of my published stories."[10] Garrett's more traditionally realistic stories make up the majority of these stories and fall into various groupings. There are stories of initiation and growing up ("The Rivals," "King of the Mountain," "The Lion Hunter," "The Test," "The Seacoast of Bohemia," "The Last of the Spanish Blood," "In the Briar Patch"). There are stories of the tensions and conflicts between men and women (especially the stories grouped under the title "Four Women" in *King of the Mountain*) which are remarkable for their use of the woman's point of view and their sensitivity to that point of view. There are many stories concerning the Singletree family which relate to the novel *The Finished Man* ("King of the Mountain," "Bread From Stones," "Sweeter Than the Flesh of Birds"). There

POEMS AND SHORT STORIES

are the army stories, and there are stories concerned directly with art and the imagination which, while still realistic, take on distinctly parabolic qualities ("An Evening Performance," "Goodbye, Good-bye, Be Always Kind and True," "A Wreath for Garibaldi," "What's the Matter with Mary Jane?").

In addition to all the realistic stories there are stories that are clearly modeled on medieval *fabliaux* ("The Con Man," "Farmer in the Dell," "Song of a Drowning Sailor")—stories which partake of the sheer wonder and delight of pure storytelling. Even more strikingly different are the enigmatic stories, which have much of the quality of strangeness and ambiguous significance of the stories of Franz Kafka—profoundly unsettling stories ("The Witness," "The Accursed Huntsman," "How the Last War Ended," "Time of Bitter Children," "Lion," and especially "Wounded Soldier"). In them, and in such stories as "And So Love Came to Alfred Zeer" and "The Insects Are Winning," Garrett tests the boundaries of the traditional story, pressing the reader into new imaginative commitments and into an examination of the very nature of story-telling, of the relationship of the printed text to the world in which it exists. By doing away with the familiar and comfortable illusions of realistic fiction, he moves into those fictive realms beyond thematic paraphrase where the creation of meaning as a shared act between reader and author becomes itself the subject of the story. The gains Garrett and his readers make in these stories are ample preparation for the aesthetic complexities of the later novels: *Death of the Fox, The Succession,* and *Poison Pen.*

The story "A Wreath for Garibaldi" offers an example of the subtlety of Garrett's examination of the imagination and of his uses of fictional form. The story takes the form of a memoir; in its appearance in *An Evening Performance,* Garrett even calls it "A True Story" (307). In it he tells of his time in Rome, of an afternoon spent in the company of "an artist, an Italian princess, another translator, an expatriate gentleman from Mobile, Alabama, who writes poems about monkeys" (307). Against a background of worry about a resurgence of fascism in Italy, the conversation moves to the laying of a wreath on the thirtieth of April on Garibaldi's monument and flowers on the bust of Lauro di Bosis, the quixotic poet who, without really knowing how to fly an airplane, "flew over Rome one day during the early days of Mussolini and scattered leaflets across the city, denouncing the Fascists. He was never heard of again" (312). Garrett confesses his mixed feelings about Di Bosis, thinking of the people who were

POEMS AND SHORT STORIES

tortured and died dirtily and anonymously for resistance to fascism and for whom "there are few, if any wreaths" (312). For complex and faintly absurd political reasons the wreath is not laid, but Garrett does find the bust of Di Bosis and does come to understand the value of his act and its relationship to the anonymous suffering that followed it:

It was a forlorn, foolish, adolescent gesture. But it was a kind of beginning. If Mussolini was really a sensitive man, and history seems to indicate that he must have been (perhaps to his own dismay), then he heard death, however faintly, the flat sound of it—like a fly trapped in a room. I looked at Lauro di Bosis for a moment with some of the feelings usually attributed to young girls standing at the grave of Keats (318).

But the story does not end there. Garrett goes on to tell a "very simple, nonsymbolic" dream in which he tries to take a bouquet of flowers to the bust of Lauro di Bosis, cannot find the bust, and then does find it, covered with a mountain of flowers. "In my dream," he says, "I wept for shame. But I woke then and I laughed out loud and slept soundly after that" (318). The flowers for Di Bosis, Garrett's homage to bravery and symbolic gestures in a stupid and brutally absurd world, are never delivered, not on the thirtieth of April nor in the dream (except that in the dream the bust is heaped with the flowers of others), but the story itself is both a bouquet for Di Bosis and a wreath for Garibaldi. Fact and dream are joined and given larger, tangible form in the "true story" of the fiction. The memoir reveals itself, then, as something more than a memory, and as something more than just a story; it becomes itself a brave and symbolic gesture, one in which the reader may fully share.

The short fiction of George Garrett is of such high quality (and of such quantity) as to deserve a separate full-length critical study. It and the poetry are significant and important additions to Garrett's work and to literature itself, further evidence of his energy and power, of the full commitment of his serious imagination.

Notes

1. George Garrett, *James Jones* (New York: Harcourt Brace Jovanovich 1984) 23.
2. Garrett, *Enchanted Ground* (York, ME: Old Gaol Museum Press, 1981) 50.
3. Harry and Michael Medved, *The Golden Turkey Awards* (New York: Putnam's, 1980) 213.
4. David R. Slavitt, "George Garrett, Professional," *Michigan Quarterly Review* (1986): 218.

POEMS AND SHORT STORIES

5. John Hall Wheelock, "Introductory Essay: To Recapture Delight," *Poets of Today IV* (New York: Scribner's, 1957) 10.

6. Garrett, *James Jones* 23.

7. *The Collected Poems of George Garrett* (Fayetteville: University of Arkansas Press, 1984) 14–15. Further references will be noted parenthetically.

8. Wheelock 10.

9. Garrett, *For a Bitter Season* (Columbia: University of Missouri Press, 1967) 107.

10. Garrett, *An Evening Performance* (Garden City: Doubleday, 1985) ix. Further references will be noted parenthetically.

CONCLUSION

"When I was young and proud and poor and feisty," George Garrett wrote in 1985, "and such things seemed to matter, I was vain about my independence, eager to be, if I could, like Mr. Faulkner, *the cat who walks alone*. . . . And so, from time to time, I paid a price for the privilege of my freedom."[1] Independent, not from youthful vanity but because of the integrity of his fully committed imagination, Garrett has walked alone in his career in the sense that he has written what he has always chosen to write, ignoring the dictates of literary fashion and the demands of the marketplace. His interest in the historical novel and what it can reveal about the essential nature of human experience led him to re-create and give new life to the form at a time when it was almost totally ignored on the "literary scene." He has maintained his serious dedication to the writing of poetry and short fiction, even while his reputation was developing as an important novelist. He has taken chances as an essayist and critic by daring to

CONCLUSION

point a revealing finger at the emperor's new clothes, no matter what powerful literary figure was wearing them at the time. He has written a body of seriously Christian art at a time when Christian belief is too often worn on literary sleeves rather than in writers' hearts. Recognizing both that people must learn "to lie a little and live together" in this world of lies and that the complex lie of art may be the surest way of speaking the truth in such a world, Garrett has truly gone his own way, and those who have benefited most are his readers, for he has shared with them an intensive and vital imaginative experience.

The price he has had to pay is that, for all the extraordinarily high quality of his work as a poet and as a writer of fictions long and short, he has never received the general approbation of the literary world and has remained, for all of his success, an outsider. Despite the recent substantial collections of his poetry and short fiction, too much of his major work remains out of print and unmentioned in important critical surveys. This loss is shared by his readers and potential readers. His place in future accounts of twentieth-century literature, however, seems secure, for he has done too much to extend and enrich the possibilities of poetry and fiction to be long ignored.

UNDERSTANDING GEORGE GARRETT

Note

1. *The Fugitives, the Agrarians and Other Twentieth-Century Writers* (Charlottesville: Alderman Library, University of Virginia, 1985) 22.

BIBLIOGRAPHY

Books by George Garrett

The Reverend Ghost: Poems. Poets of Today IV. Ed. John Hall Wheelock. New York: Scribner's, 1957.

King of the Mountain. New York: Scribner's, 1957; London: Eyre and Spottiswoode, 1959.

The Sleeping Gypsy and Other Poems. Austin: University of Texas Press, 1958.

The Finished Man. New York: Scribner's, 1959; London: Eyre and Spottiswoode, 1960.

Abraham's Knife and Other Poems. Chapel Hill: University of North Carolina Press, 1961.

In the Briar Patch. Austin: University of Texas Press, 1961.

Which Ones Are the Enemy? Boston: Little, Brown, 1961: London: W. H. Allen, 1962.

Sir Slob and the Princess: A Play for Children. New York: Samuel French, 1962.

Cold Ground Was My Bed Last Night. Columbia: University of Missouri Press, 1964.

Do, Lord, Remember Me. London: Chapman and Hall, 1965; Garden City: Doubleday, 1965.

For a Bitter Season: New and Selected Poems. Columbia: University of Missouri Press, 1967.

A Wreath for Garibaldi and Other Stories. London: Rupert Hart-Davis, 1969.

Death of the Fox. Garden City: Doubleday, 1971; London: Barrie and Jenkins, 1972.

The Magic Striptease. Garden City: Doubleday, 1973.

Welcome to the Medicine Show: Flashcards / Postcards / Snapshots. Winston-Salem, NC: Palaemon Press, 1978.

To Recollect a Cloud of Ghosts: Christmas in England 1602–1603. Winston-Salem, NC: Palaemon Press, 1980.

Luck's Shining Child: A Miscellany of Poems & Verses. Winston-Salem, NC: Palaemon Press, 1981.

BIBLIOGRAPHY

Enchanted Ground: A Play for Readers' Theater. York, ME: Old Gaol Museum Press, 1981.

The Succession: A Novel of Elizabeth and James. Garden City: Doubleday, 1983.

The Collected Poems of George Garrett. Fayetteville: University of Arkansas Press, 1984.

James Jones. New York: Harcourt Brace Jovanovich, 1984.

An Evening Performance: New and Selected Short Stories. Garden City: Doubleday, 1985.

Poison Pen; or, Live Now and Pay Later. Winston-Salem, NC: Stuart Wright, 1986.

Understanding Mary Lee Settle. Columbia: University of South Carolina Press, 1988.

Books Edited by Garrett

New Writing from Virginia. Charlottesville: New Writing Associates, 1963.

The Girl in the Black Raincoat. New York: Duell, Sloan and Pearce, 1966.

Man and the Movies. Ed. W. R. Robinson "with assistance by George Garrett." Baton Rouge: Louisiana State University Press, 1967.

New Writing in South Carolina (with William Peden). Columbia: University of South Carolina Press, 1971.

Film Scripts One (with Jane Gelfman and O. B. Hardison). New York: Appleton-Century, 1971.

The Sounder Few: Selected Essays from "The Hollins Critic" (with R. H. W. Dillard and John Rees Moore). Athens: University of Georgia Press, 1971.

Film Scripts Two (with Jane Gelfman and O. B. Hardison). New York: Appleton-Century, 1971.

BIBLIOGRAPHY

Film Scripts Three (with Jane Gelfman and O. B. Hardison). New York: Appleton-Century, 1972.

Film Scripts Four (with Jane Gelfman and O. B. Hardison). New York: Appleton-Century, 1972.

Craft So Hard to Learn: Conversations with Poets and Writers about the Teaching of Writing. Interviews conducted by John Graham. New York: Morrow, 1972.

The Writer's Voice: Conversations with Contemporary Writers. Interviews conducted by John Graham. New York: Morrow, 1973.

Intro 5 (with Walton Beacham). Charlottesville: University Press of Virginia, 1974.

Botteghe Oscure Reader (with Katherine Garrison Biddle). Middletown: Wesleyan University Press, 1974.

Intro 6: Life as We Know It. Garden City: Doubleday, 1974.

Intro 7: All of Us and None of You. Garden City: Doubleday, 1975.

Intro 8: The Liar's Craft. Garden City: Doubleday, 1977.

Intro 9: Close to Home. Austin: Hendel and Reinke, 1978.

Unpublished Play and Screenplays by Garrett

Garden Spot, U.S.A. Two-act comedy; opened the Alley Theatre, Houston, 25 April 1962.

The Young Lovers. Screenplay based on the novel by Julian Halevy. Produced and directed by Samuel Goldwyn, Jr. MGM, 1965.

The Playground. Screenplay based on *My Brother, Death,* by Cyrus Sulzberger. Produced and directed by Richard Hilliard. Jerand, 1965.

Frankenstein Meets the Space Monster. Original screenplay by Garrett, R. H. W. Dillard, and John Rodenbeck. A Vernon production, directed by Robert Gaffney. Allied Artists, 1965.

Selected Essays by Garrett

"An Examination of the Poetry of William Faulkner." *Princeton University Library Chronicle* 18 (1957): 124-35.

"*By Love Possessed:* The Pattern and the Hero." *Critique* 1 (1958): 41-47.

"The Function of the Pasiphae Myth in *Brother to Dragons.*" *Modern Language Notes* 74 (1959): 311-13.

"The Major Poetry of Joyce Cary." *Modern Fiction Studies* 9 (1963): 245-56.

"One Kind of Anarchy." *College English* 25 (1963): 163-69.

"John Cheever and the Charms of Innocence." *Hollins Critic* 1 (1964): 1-12.

"Against the Grain: Poets Writing Today." *American Poetry.* Ed. Irvin Ehrenpreis. London: Edward Arnold, 1965. 221-39.

"Don't Make Waves." *Man and the Movies.* Ed. W. R. Robinson and George Garrett. Baton Rouge: Louisiana State University Press, 1966. 227-60.

"A New Look at William Faulkner." *Shenandoah* 18 (1966): 93-99.

"Morris the Magician: A Look at *In Orbit*." *Hollins Critic* 4 (1967): 1-12.

"An Open Letter from George Garrett." *toward winter.* Ed. Harry Nash and Robert Bonazzi. Houston: Latitudes Press, 1968. 35-49.

"Dreaming with Adam: Notes on Imaginary History." *New Literary History* 1 (1970): 407-21.

"Teaching Writing: A Letter to the Editor." *Writers as Teachers,*

BIBLIOGRAPHY

Teachers as Writers. Ed. Jonathan Baumbach. New York: Holt, Rinehart and Winston, 1970. 59–75.

"Notes on *The Playground.*" *Mill Mountain Review* 1 (1971): 51–52.

"Ladies in Boston *Have* Their Hats: Notes on WASP Humor." *Comic Relief: Humor in Contemporary American Fiction.* Ed. Sara Blacher Cohen. Urbana: University of Illinois Press, 1978. 207–37.

"Whatever Wishful Thinking May Wish: The Example of James Gould Cozzens." *Just Representations: A James Gould Cozzens Reader.* Ed. Matthew J. Bruccoli. Carbondale: Southern Illinois University Press; New York: Harcourt Brace Jovanovich, 1978. 197–203.

"Plain and/or Fancy: Where the Short Story Is and May Be Going." *The Teller and the Tale: Aspects of the Short Story.* Ed. Wendell M. Aycock. Lubbock: Texas Tech Press, 1982. 133–41.

"In the Absence of a Manifesto." *Bennington Review* 16 (1984): 4–6.

"How to Do the Literary." *Voicelust: Eight Contemporary Fiction Writers on Style.* Ed. Allen Wier and Don Hendrie, Jr. Lincoln: University of Nebraska Press, 1985. 67–86.

"Daily Life in City, Town, and County." *William Shakespeare: His World, His Work, His Influence.* Ed. John F. Andrews. New York: Scribner's, 1985. 1: 215–32.

" 'Fix My Hair, Jack': The Dark Side of Faulkner's Jokes." *Faulkner and Humor.* Ed. Doreen Fowler and Ann J. Abadie. Jackson: University Press of Mississippi, 1986. 216–31.

"My Two One-Eyed Coaches." *An Apple for My Teacher: Twelve Authors Tell about Teachers Who Made the Difference.* Ed. Louis D. Rubin, Jr. Chapel Hill, NC: Algonquin Books, 1987. 77–114.

BIBLIOGRAPHY

Interviews

Carr, John. "Kite-Flying and Other Irrational Acts: George Garrett." *Kite-Flying and Other Irrational Acts: Conversations with Twelve Southern Writers.* Baton Rouge: Louisiana State University Press, 1972. 174–98.

Graham, John. "Fiction and Film: An Interview with George Garrett." *Film Journal* 1 (1971): 22–25.

———. and W. R. Robinson. "George Garrett Discusses Writing and His Work." *Mill Mountain Review* 1 (1971): 79–102.

"An Interview with George Garrett." *Dictionary of Literary Biography Yearbook: 1983.* Ed. Mary Bruccoli and Jean W. Ross. Detroit: Gale, 1984. 157–61.

Israel, Charles. "Interview: George Garrett." *South Carolina Review* 4 (1973): 43–48.

Wier, Allen. "An Interview with George Garrett." *Penny Dreadful* 4 (1975): 13–18.

———. "George Garrett." *Transatlantic Review* 58/59 (1977): 58–61.

Critical Articles about Garrett

Israel, Charles. "George Garrett." *American Poets Since World War II.* Vol. 5 of *Dictionary of Literary Biography.* Ed. Donald J. Greiner. Detroit: Bruccoli Clark / Gale, 1980. 264–69. Overview of the development of Garrett's poetry.

Mill Mountain Review 1 (1971). Special issue in appreciation of George Garrett. Ed. Irv Broughton and R. H. W. Dillard. Contains, in addition to an interview and excerpts from work in progress, essays and appreciations by, among others, Joseph Blotner, R. V. Cassill, Fred Chappell, Louis O. Coxe, Babette Deutsch, Brewster Ghiselin, Daniel Hoffman, Gordon Lish, David Madden, William Jay Smith,

BIBLIOGRAPHY

Walter Sullivan, Henry Taylor, James Whitehead, and Richard Wilbur.

Peden, William. "The Short Fiction of George Garrett." *Ploughshares* 4 (1978): 83-90. Overview of Garrett's short fiction emphasizing his experimental and innovative search for form and method to achieve the right and inevitable marriage of subject matter and structure.

Rhodes, Jack Wright. "George Garrett." *American Novelists Since World War II.* Vol. 2 of *Dictionary of Literary Biography.* Ed. Jeffrey Helterman and Richard Layman. Detroit: Bruccoli Clark / Gale, 1978. 185-90. Overview of Garrett's fiction especially in light of the development of his technique.

Robinson, W. R. "Imagining the Individual: George Garrett's *Death of the Fox.*" *Hollins Critic* 8 (1971): 1-12. Reading of Garrett's novels, especially *Death of the Fox,* as celebrations of the imagination that acts to incarnate what it values.

———. "The Fiction of George Garrett." *Red Clay Reader* 2 (1965): 15-16. Reading of Garrett's first three novels and short fiction as explorations of change through the lives of individuals who are simultaneously free and responsible, empowered but moral.

Slavitt, David R. "George Garrett, Professional." *Michigan Quarterly Review* (1986): 218-25. Examination of the interrelationship of Garrett's poetry and short fiction.

———. "History—Fate and Freedom: A Look at George Garrett's New Novel." *Southern Review* 7 (1971): 276-94. Account of the genesis of *Death of the Fox* in the context of Garrett's work.

Spears, Monroe K. "George Garrett and the Historical Novel." *Virginia Quarterly Review* 61 (1985): 262-76. Rpt. *American Ambitions: Selected Essays on Literary and Cultural Things.* Baltimore: Johns Hopkins University Press, 1987.

200-10. Argues that Garrett's historical novels are as fully historical as they are modern, both repudiations of and fulfillments of the genre.

Taylor, Henry. "The Poetry of George Garrett." *Latitudes* 2 (1968): 30-31. Argues that Garrett's poetry is fully as important as his fiction.

Whalen, Tom. "The Reader Becomes Text: Methods of Experimentation in George Garrett's *The Succession: A Novel of Elizabeth and James.*" *Texas Review* 4 (1983): 14-21. Analysis of *The Succession* as a mannerist work which uses a full range of experimental techniques to make the past palpable to its readers.

Wheelock, John Hall. "Introductory Essay: To Recapture Delight." *Poets of Today IV.* New York: Scribner's, 1957. 3-17. Description of Garrett's early poems as strangely musical but almost tormented approaches to the essence of things.

Bibliographies

Dillard, R. H. W. "George Garrett: A Checklist of His Writings." *Mill Mountain Review* 1 (1971): 221-34.

Meriwether, James B. "George Palmer Garrett." *Seven Princeton Poets.* Ed. Sherman Hawkes. Princeton: Princeton University Library, 1963. 26-39.

———. "George Garrett." *First Printings of American Authors.* Detroit: Gale, 1976. 2: 167-73.

Wright, Stuart. "George Garrett: A Bibliographical Chronicle, 1947-1980." *Bulletin of Bibliography* 38 (1980): 6-19, 25.

INDEX

The index does not include references to material in the notes.

Abraham, 26
Andress, Ursula, 167, 183
Ann-Margret, 8, 167
Apsley, Sir Allan, 121, 130
Aristophanes, 177
Auden, W. H., 137
Augustine, Saint, 22, 198

Bacon, Sir Francis, 121-122, 131-132, 173
Barnes, Djuna: *Ryder,* 117
Barth, Karl, 19, 21, 24, 92
Bible, 12, 18, 26-27, 67-68, 91, 97, 99, 201-202, 203
Biddle, Livingston, 183
Booth, Wayne C., 185
Borges, Jorge Luis, 132
Bosch, Hieronymus, 102-103; *Garden of Earthly Delights,* 102
Brady, Matthew, 36, 39
Brandon, Gregory, 122
Brinkley, Christie, 167, 176, 185-188, 190
Bunyan, John, 96

Caedmon, 23, 200
Caldwell, Erskine: *Journeyman,* 180
Camus, Albert, 189
Canons of Hippolytus, 91
Capote, Truman, 183, 185
Carey, Robert, earl of Monmouth, 141, 150
Carter, Jimmy, 183
Cary, Joyce, 193
Cecil, Sir Robert, 141, 144, 150, 152-153, 157

INDEX

Cecil, William, 143, 146
Charles I, king, 113
Chaucer, Geoffrey, 6, 81, 87-88, 104, 165; *The Canterbury Tales,* 87, 90, 200
Cortázar, Julio: *Hopscotch,* 149
Cozzens, James Gould, 193-194

D'Annunzio, Gabriele, 178
Dante Alighieri: *Inferno,* 58
Defoe, Daniel: *The Shortest Way with Dissenters,* 165
Delilah, 99
DeLorean, Mrs. John, 183
Di Bosis, Lauro, 206-208
Duse, Eleanora, 178

Eco, Umberto, 29-30, 150
Einstein, Albert, 129, 144
Elizabeth I, queen, 7, 12, 113-161 *passim,* 164
Essex, earl of, 141, 144, 146-147, 155, 156
Eve, 96, 101, 200

Farmer, James, 183
Faulkner, William, 6, 55, 112, 193, 203, 210; *As I Lay Dying,* 85
Fellini, Federico, 184, 188
Fielding, Henry, 81
FitzGerald, Edward, 132, 134
Fitzgerald, F. Scott, 194
Fleming, Thomas, 177
Foster, Jody, 184
Frye, Northrop, 17, 100

Gardner, Brother Dave, 174
Garibaldi, Giuseppe, 206-208
Garrett, George: career of, 1-4

INDEX

Critical Biography
James Jones, 193, 198
Novels
Death of the Fox, 3, 5, 7, 12, 18, 112-139, 141, 142, 161, 163, 173, 186, 190, 195, 206; "Stars Must Fall," 114-115, 133-135
Do, Lord, Remember Me, 3, 6, 12-13, 79-110, 112, 127, 166, 174, 179, 194
The Finished Man, 3, 5-6, 8, 16, 29, 34-55, 112, 163, 164, 204
Poison Pen, 2, 3, 8, 13, 29, 30, 108, 139, 163-191, 194, 196, 206; *Life With Kim Novak Is Hell*, 8, 174, 175-176, 181, 190
The Succession, 3, 6, 12, 29, 30, 112-120, 139, 139-161, 163-164, 186, 190, 195, 206
Which Ones Are the Enemy?, 3, 6, 13, 57-78, 112
Plays
Enchanted Ground, 194-195
Garden Spot, U.S.A., 194
Sir Slob and the Princess, 194
Poetry
Abraham's Knife, 3, 19
"Abraham's Knife," 200, 203
"Angels," 23
"Caedmon," 200
"Celebrity Verses," 8, 167, 200
"Child Among Ancestors," 10-11
The Collected Poems of George Garrett, 4, 168
"Congreve," 200
"Consolations of Philosophy," 169
"Crows at Paestum," 200
"Easter," 170
"An Epigram by Martial," 202-203
"Eve," 200
"Fig Leaves," 19-20, 203
"Flashcards," 168, 200
"For a Bitter Season," 11, 199
For a Bitter Season, 8

INDEX

"For My Sons," 17-18, 136-137, 203
"Forsythia," 201
"Four American Landscapes," 11
"From the Academy," 200
"Gadfly," 166
"General Prologue," 200
"Holy Roller," 89-90
"I Must Have Peaked Too Early," 169
"In Tuscany," 200
"Invitation," 200
"Jacob," 169
"Luck's Shining Child," 14, 203
"Main Currents of American Political Thought," 11, 34-35, 54
"Maine Weathers," 11-12, 200, 203
"The March Problem," 201
"Matthew Arnold," 200
"Meditation on Romans," 12, 201-202, 203
"Milksop, the Poetaster," 166
"Old Slavemarket: St. Augustine, Fla." 200
"Out on the Circuit," 203
"Percé Rock," 200
"Portrait of the Artist as a Cartoon," 169
The Reverend Ghost, 2, 197
"Revival," 88-89
"Rugby Road," 202, 203
"Salome," 11, 13, 21, 200, 203
"Shards for Her," 200
"Since It Is Valentine's Day," 200
The Sleeping Gypsy, 166
"Some Women," 200, 203
"Swift," 200
"Three Characters in Search of a New Dunciad," 200
"Tiresias," 200
"To a Certain Critic," 168
"To a Rival Poet," 168

INDEX

"Welcome to the Medicine Show," 168
Short Fiction
"The Accursed Huntsman," 5, 205
"And So Love Came to Alfred Zeer," 166, 205
"The Blood of Strangers," 59
"Bread From Stones," 204
"Cold Ground Was My Bed Last Night" (see "Noise of Strangers")
Cold Ground Was My Bed Last Night, 59
"Comic Strip," 5
"The Con Man," 205
"Don't Take No for an Answer," 59, 73-74
"An Evening Performance," 25-28, 205
An Evening Performance, 4, 16, 80, 204, 206
"Farmer in the Dell," 166, 205
"Four Women," 204
"Good-bye, Good-bye, Be Always Kind and True," 205
"A Hard Row to Hoe," 41
"Hooray for the Old Nth Field," 14
"How the Last War Ended," 5, 59, 205
"In the Briar Patch," 204
In the Briar Patch, 3, 41
"The Insects Are Winning," 205
"Jane Amor, Space Nurse," 174-175
"King of the Mountain," 15, 41-43, 52, 204
King of the Mountain, 2, 5, 41, 57, 59, 203, 204
"The Last of the Spanish Blood," 16, 204
"Lion," 41, 205
"The Lion Hunter," 16, 204
"The Magic Striptease," 170-174
The Magic Striptease, 30, 80
"Noise of Strangers," 16-17, 80, 81-85, 103, 106
"The Old Army Game," 59, 61-62
"A Record as Long as Your Arm," 175, 176, 179, 189-190
"The Rivals," 16, 203-204
"The Satyr Shall Cry," 80, 103-109, 166

INDEX

"The Seacoast of Bohemia," 16, 41, 55, 204
"Song of a Drowning Sailor," 205
"Sweeter Than the Flesh of Birds," 204
"The Test," 204
"Texarkana Was a Crazy Town," 59-61
"Three Fabliaux," 165-166
"Time of Bitter Children," 205
To Recollect a Cloud of Ghosts, 195
"To Whom Shall I Turn Now in My Hour of Need," 80
"Torment,"57-58
"Unmapped Country," 59
"What's the Matter with Mary Jane?" 205
"What's the Purpose of the Bayonet?" 5, 14, 57, 59, 204
"The Witness," 5, 205
"Wounded Soldier," 59, 205
"A Wreath for Garibaldi," 205, 206-208
A Wreath for Garibaldi, 80
Screenplays
Frankenstein Meets the Space Monster, 196
The Playground, 195-196
The Young Lovers, 195
Garrett, Susan Parrish Jackson, 2, 188-189
Golding, Arthur: translation of Ovid's *Metamorphosis*, 142
Goldwater, Barry, 177, 183
Goldwyn, Samuel, Jr., 195
Gorky, Maxim: *Bystanders*, 61-62
Graham, Billy, 94
Graham, John, 8

Hall, Joseph, 165
Hefner, Hugh, 183, 184
Hemingway, Ernest, 5, 112, 203; *A Farewell to Arms*, 75; *To Have and Have Not*, 65
Henry VIII, king, 123-124
Hill School, 2

INDEX

Hilliard, Richard, 195
Hollins College, 2
Holofernes, 99

Isaiah, 65, 67, 97
Israel, Charles, 10, 29

Jacob, 23, 26, 169
James I, king (James VI of Scotland), 7, 113, 117, 121, 129-130, 132, 140-161 *passim*
Jeremiah, 65
Jesus Christ, 12, 15, 24, 30, 76, 87, 93-94, 100, 138, 170, 201-202
Job, 65, 68
Joel, Billy, 187
Johnson, B. S.: *The Unfortunates*, 149
Johnson, Lyndon, 183
Jones, James, 1, 58, 193
Joyce, James: *Finnegans Wake*, 117; *Ulysses*, 2
Judas, 138
Judith, 99
Juvenal, 165

Kafka, Franz, 205
Katzenbach, Maria, 169
Kennedy, John F., 53
Kennedy, Robert, 183
Kennedy, Teddy, 183
Khayyám, Omar, 132, 134
Ku Klux Klan, 39-41, 48

Leicester, earl of, 155
Lewis, Sinclair: *Elmer Gantry*, 3
Lilith, 97, 101
Lish, Gordon: *Dear Mr. Capote*, 185

INDEX

Lovelace, Linda, 183
Lucilius, 165

Macpherson, Aimee Semple, 170
Magna Mater, 95
Mailer, Norman: *Ancient Evenings*, 113
Martial, 193
Mary, queen, 124
Mary, Magdalene, 96
Mary Queen of Scots, 148
Masters and Johnson, 183
Medved, Harry and Michael, 196
Mencken, H. L., 177
Michell, Donna, 8, 167
Mithra, 95
Mussolini, Benito, 207

Nabokov, Vladimir: *Pale Fire*, 149
Noah, 99
Novak, Kim, 8, 167

Overbury, Sir Thomas, 122

Paul, Saint, 90
Persius, 165
Philistines, 52
Pike, Bishop James, 183
Pilate, 83–84
Pope, Alexander, 165
Princeton University, 2, 22, 115

Rabelais, François, 177
Ralegh, Carew, 18, 135
Ralegh, Sir Walter, 7, 12, 18, 115–139 *passim*, 155
Reagan, Ronald, 177, 183

INDEX

Reed, Kit, 163
Rhodes, Jack Wright, 65
Robertson, D. W., Jr., 22-23
Robinson, W. R., 13, 15, 44, 135

Salinger, J. D., 112; *The Catcher in the Rye*, 66-67
Salome, 11, 13, 21, 46-47, 96, 200, 203
Samson, 52, 99
Sartre, Jean-Paul, 189
Satan, 28
Scott, Sir Walter: *Kenilworth*, 155; *Waverly*, 113
Scribners, 6
Settle, Mary Lee, 1
Sewanee Military Academy, 2
Shakespeare, William, 158
Shields, Brooke, 167, 183-184
Shrimpton, Jean, 183
Sitwell, Edith: *Fanfare for Elizabeth*, 116
Slavitt, David R., 197
Socrates, 126
Solomon, 70
Southern, Terry: *The Magic Christian*, 183
Spears, Monroe K., 2, 7, 113, 118-119, 143, 144-145
Steele, Barbara, 8, 167
Steenie (George Villiers, duke of Buckingham), 130
Stein, Gertrude, 120, 188; *Tender Buttons*, 140
Stevens, Wallace, 134; "No Possum, No Sop, No Taters," 84-85
Stevenson, Adlai E., 35, 53
Strand, Mark, 175
Stukely, Sir Lewis, 131, 138
Swift, Jonathan, 165, 200

Tiegs, Cheryl, 167, 183
Tolstoy, Lev, 158

INDEX

Twain, Mark, 177, 180; *A Connecticut Yankee in King Arthur's Court,* 170; *The Mysterious Stranger,* 170
Twiggy, 8, 167

University of Michigan, 2
University of South Carolina, 2
University of Virginia, 3, 186, 196
Updike, John, 175

Wallace, George, 183
Warhol, Andy, 171
Warren, Robert Penn, 55, 112, 194; *All the King's Men,* 6
Wesleyan University, 2
Wheelock, John Hall, 197, 200
Whitman, Walt, 171
Williams, Charles, 91
Willingham, Calder: *Eternal Fire,* 180
Wilson, Clyde, 177
Wilson, Sir Thomas, 130

Yeats, William Butler: "Dialogue of Self and Soul," 51
Yelverton, Henry, 121
Yourcenar, Marguerite: *Hadrian's Memoirs,* 116